FriesenPress

Suite 300 - 990 Fort St
Victoria, BC, V8V 3K2
Canada

www.friesenpress.com

ISBN
978-1-5255-4582-5 (Hardcover)
978-1-5255-4583-2 (Paperback)
978-1-5255-4584-9 (eBook)

1. SELF-HELP, MOTIVATIONAL & INSPIRATIONAL

Distributed to the trade by The Ingram Book Company

THE
FLIGHT
OF THE
PHOENIX

Living Forward

H.B. PIERRE SIMON JR.

PREFACE
"AN AUTHOR'S PLEA"

The power and history behind one of the world's most mystical creatures—the phoenix—is one that has taken many different shapes and forms throughout history. Though Greek mythology, Persian tales, Egyptian legends, and Roman folklore all lay claim to the inception of this mythical bird, the one thing that remains constant throughout these varying perspectives is that all ancient discussions lead to the general consensus that the phoenix stood for renewal, rebirth, strength, and in most cases immortality. But unlike creatures from your other fairy tales, the phoenix achieved this level of reverence throughout history by staring the ultimate challenge in the face and defeating it; death. This magnificent creature, though of course mythological, has been passed down through the generations as being the fiercest yet most beautiful fowl to ever soar the lower heavens. With razor sharp, spear-like talons and its large wingspan, the phoenix closely resembles the Greek's revered *Haliaeetus Leucocephalus*, the modern-day bald eagle. With an array of feathers adorned with dazzling shades of gold, accompanied by a fiery-red, diamond-cut upper plumage, the phoenix ruled the skies. Born through fire, its wings and its tail would carry on this ignition for the entirety of its lifespan burning larger in size during flight. An absolutely amazing creation, the phoenix possessed sight as keen as a hawk and soul-piercing eyes as intense as an eagle's, yet it was said to be as gentle as a sparrow. According to historians, the phoenix had a life span of at least five hundred years, where thereafter it would prepare itself for its violent, fiery death. Though to some this sudden ignition into flames cannot be seen as strength, renewal, rebirth, or immortality, to the phoenix, this critical transition from life to a seemingly fiery grave was vital and necessary in order to achieve its rebirth from the ashes. Its unorthodox rebirth might be seen as a process that breaks the very thought of status quo and every other normality.

After five hundred years, the phoenix would prepare itself for its moment of tumultuous demise by building a nest within an oak or palm tree just prior to its transition. Once all had been prepared, the bird would violently burst into flames, utterly destroying every portion of its existence. Its entire spectacle of perfectly-cut trim of feathers in all of its beauty would be engulfed and destroyed within a furnace of necessity. Then it would happen! Something amazing would occur! From its own ashes the once-deceased creature would then be reborn. Through this transition the phoenix not only received its reputation for immortality, but the mystical creature now lived the next stint of its life stronger, wiser, and more powerful than ever before, dominating the skies until the necessary sacrifice was upon it again.

This life cycle is also what provided the phoenix with its immortality within history. Passed down from generation to generation, the tale of this fiery bird has captured the hearts of many because of its figurative resemblance to the struggles and continual challenges we mortal humans face while here on earth. But just as the phoenix accepts his fiery fate, it is not for us to regret and deny the inevitable, but rather to learn to embrace it that we too may be reborn, renewed, and strengthened, undyingly facing our daily obstacles.

Amongst all species on earth, there has never been another creature figurative or literal, which was born out of such a tumultuous process. Because of this, I draw a parallel to our lives. In order to receive a similar reverence, respect, and rebirth throughout our own journeys, we too must step outside of the status quo and stand face to face with our most difficult obstacles.

What is most interesting to me is that according to mythology, during ignition and burning, every single part of the bird, including its talons, feathers, and bones was completely consumed by this violent fire. My hope is that after reading this book, we will all understand that when we are enhancing our lives for the better, at times we have to let go of everything and completely start over. This may mean leaving behind the good, displacing all that we once possessed, and retraining our minds and ideals, in hopes of achieving a greater existence.

I draw the parallel between this mystical creature and our lives not to sound crafty in naming a novel. Rather, I chose the phoenix because my prayer for each of you is that you not only be strengthened through perseverance against your obstacles and reborn through the fiery trials and misfortunes of life, but more importantly that the story of "YOU" can be passed down from generation to generation. I say passed down, because just like the phoenix, you awakened daily, walked your own journeys, faced your inevitabilities in life, thoroughly prepared yourself for each "next step" of life, and beat what seemed to be "all odds against you" or your own figurative "fiery grave."

My plea is for each of you to read the words of this book diligently and honestly that you may, in turn, take flight and soar, ruling your skies, your lives, and your lower heavens, just like the magnificent phoenix.

Throughout this book we will delve into many of the things that are common throughout our journeys in life. What I'd ask each of you to do is open your hearts that we may all grow together.

Originally inspired by a true event, which I happened to witness, *Flight of the Phoenix* will allow us to change our focus from what we can't control to what we can. We will take a look at the time, years, and focus we have spent on things that only hinder us from reaching our full potential in life. We will learn from the past but focus on the present that we may live a better future. Unlike what might be true in most "self-help" books, I won't dare exclude the fact that the majority of our problems in life come from our biggest adversary... OURSELVES... Because of this fact, we will figure out how to get out of our own way to continue down our journey. During our flight to immortality we'll also deal with defeat and the overcoming of said defeat. This is important because defeat is inevitable at some point, but how we deal with it will determine if we'll go down in history as the phoenix or if we'll allow our flames of life to engulf and consume us, never to rise again.

Later in our flight, we will shed light on the fact that as long as there is breath within our lungs, we possess a fighting chance at life despite all it has to throw our way. This is not to say that our obstacles will always be easy to overcome—in fact, at times they will feel like we are running marathons in quicksand or trying to fly a paper kite through the eye of a Category Five hurricane. But as we will read, pressing forward in the face of adversity, even one non-obvious step at a time, will thoroughly prepare us for our own transition from our ends to our new beginnings in life; just like the phoenix.

In closing, we will finish our flight by looking in retrospect at our new lives lived without regret. The hope is that we learn the importance of living every tick of the clock to its fullest, for it in itself is finite.

AUTHOR'S NOTE

Let us begin our journey with the true story, "The Feeding Frenzy," which originally inspired this book. I've split the story in half and I sincerely ask that you save the conclusion for its proper place…at the end of this book.

LET'S BEGIN.

THE FEEDING FRENZY

Once, while visiting Santa Cruz, California, I witnessed a lively flock of seagulls. These very anxious birds were feasting on the entrails and spoils of the day as an exhausted fisherman cleaned and separated his catch between filet and that which was to be thrown away as remains. This flock fought not only amongst each other for the rewards of the catch, but they also faced a much larger adversary, a band of seals that had sniffed out the aroma of the fresh catch. Apparently, that stench gave life to the entire harbor and all of its inhabitants.

Though initially amazed at this apparent circle of life renewing itself, my attention was drawn toward two small seagulls that stood on the outskirts of the fiasco not daring to enter lest they too be consumed amongst all the turmoil. However, there was no chivalry here, no "sharing that we all may eat," just the mere definition of everyone or every creature for themselves. As the fisherman concluded his post-catch ritual, and the spoils were thoroughly devoured, the flock of seagulls and the band of seals all began to disperse one by one until the once blood-thirsty fisherman's dock, was only occupied by the two little remaining seagulls. These two patient seagulls had remained hoping to find enough scraps to fill their empty stomachs and uplift their waiting hearts.

We have all experienced being last in our lives; the feeling of "When will it be my turn?" We've seen others around

*us excel while we seem to be running around in circles.
Hopelessness has knocked on the front door, and without the
courtesy of a "Come on in," invited itself within the confines
of our hearts.*

As the little gulls rummaged through the remains, they
stumbled upon the head of a redfish. Though there was
hardly any meat remaining, the two tiny birds began to share
their newfound meal. As one ate the other watched out for
potential larger-beaked thieves. The gulls worked in glorious harmony, eating and then on guard, all to preserve the
meager sustenance for which they had so diligently waited.
At this point all seemed as though, "The patient, in the end
get rewarded." Yet there was more to be seen. Out of nowhere
swooped down another seagull squawking and flapping its
large, spread wings. So, of course, since it was a larger size the
two smaller birds yielded their territory as well as their meal.
Empty-beaked yet again, kicked to the curb yet again—*How
will they respond?* I thought.

"When the test of patience truly becomes virtue"

We've been taught that patience is a virtue. However, we're not taught that the true virtue of patience can only be achieved when we have been patient and yet our situation still continues to spiral toward the negative. As you read and wonder how the two fowls responded, I ask you to look inside yourself and ask, *How do I respond in the face of adversity?* How do we respond when life has discarded us, when we are without direction, or when we don't know where our next meal will come from? How do we respond?

Ask yourself, *How have I responded in the past?* because hopefully, by the end of this book, that answer will be slightly altered.

You see, before we can dive into the flight of the phoenix, I implore each of you to take a second and think of your life in retrospect. Allow your mind to be at rest and begin to pull out specific instances when you too have felt like you had to stand on the outskirts while others were within the "frenzy." What situation might you be currently facing or have faced recently where you feel like you were forced to wait patiently while others around you were getting their opportunities at "Succeeding in Life"? This recollection will be vital to our journey throughout the flight, because we will take an in-depth look at the spectrum of these events. This in-depth look will start from the realization of a change needing to take place and lead to the final product of reward, due to staring your ultimate challenges in the face and defeating them.

So, open your minds, be honest with yourselves, allow the power of the phoenix to fill your hearts, and let's take this journey together.

WHAT IF VS. WHAT IS

It's amazing how two letters alone can be the difference between living in the past, thriving in the present, or excelling in the future. Because we desire to be great it is almost a natural inclination to delve into our pasts and harp on how our past mistakes, if not committed, could have bettered our present outcome. However, what we fail to realize is that if we take the same energy, time, and years that we spend dwelling on the what we can't change; the "What ifs," and transfer that energy to what we can control; the "What is," we will surpass our current progress as well overcome any failures we may have had. It is because of this I will dedicate this chapter to the things that occur in life, while transferring the focus from the "What if" to the "What is."

Are you ready? Let's Go.

"If" is defined as an uncertain possibility; something that implies a condition on which something else depends. How often do we find ourselves asking, "What if I had said this?" or "What if I hadn't done that?" The fact is, beating ourselves up over the "ifs" in life is futile because, all ifs are uncertain, which leads us down a path of wasted time and energy. Now I'd be remiss to glaze over the "ifs" as though they are unimportant. So, I must bring some clarity. It is not that these times, mistakes, and regrets in life are unimportant, but rather that we must change the way we approach them. Think about it—water is the elixir of life yet too much of it and you drown. By this I say that all things, including our reflections on the past must be had in moderation. For if too much time is spent looking into the past, how much of our existence are we missing out on, and what is there left for the present?

So how should we approach our ifs in life?

Step 1: Breathe. Recognize that unless you have a time machine, a hover board, or an old DeLorean fueled by trash, you can never go back and change what has been done. Though facetiously put, this screams to the rationale that very few things in your past can be altered, once they are done. However, what we will be focusing on is learning from the past to build a better future.

Step 2: Realize that there are a million different possible variables that could have altered your current equation.

Step 3: If your current status appears to be unfortunate due to a choice you made, then write out the situation and the choice that would have led to a better result. Also write out the poor choice you made that led to the current result. I say write it out because once you have thought of and expressed the choice you made, the road to your current status, and a potential road to success, your brain now has a three-way road map for future reference. Similar to how that road in the woods diverged for Robert Frost, your brain now can visualize a road to failure and a road to your current status, as well as a potential road to success. Now it is time for Step 4.

Step 4: Which is to learn from it and move forward. So how do we learn from our dreaded "What if" and move on? We do so by now focusing on the "What is," which is the point in life that we can actually control; THE HERE, THE NOW.

First let's dig into steps 3 and 4.

Why are we writing out our past situations and the mistakes we made at the time of failure? We need to do this because surprisingly most of the failures we find ourselves with come at the hand of our greatest enemy—ourselves. To understand this will be beneficial because it is important not only to know that we made the wrong choice, but to see and thoroughly review the situation, because often-times the situation that led to the mistake could have been avoided.

As most would agree, this commonsense aspect of seeing more clearly in hindsight would prove to be more beneficial if it were present during the heat of our battles. Therefore, noting your failure, reviewing both your wrong choice and the better choice, allows you the opportunity to review what choice or choices would have led to a better result.

While reviewing your list ask, "How could this have been avoided, and did I place myself in a position to fail?" Usually, looking back, these answers seem obvious because we're not in the heat of the moment. However, I encourage each of you to continually refer to your list until the answers that lead toward better results become a part of you, throughout and outside of the heat of the moment.

Imagine studying for a test using index cards. The difference is this exam is on the subject of life and you may see the test questions time and time again. For it is not the single presentation of a challenge that qualifies it as "Something we struggle with." Rather it is the consistent facing of and our frequent failures of said challenges that qualify them as items we "struggle with." The more you write out the correct answer or response, the more the "correct answer" will become a part of you, and you'll pick the correct answer during your exam of life.

2 + 2 = 4

Two plus two equals four. But why? How do we know this to be true? Well, it all started with our first-grade teachers or parents telling us and we took it for truth; though at the time we didn't initially know why. Later in life we had to learn all of our numbers, the counting process, and the process of addition as well as that of subtraction. This brought a little more clarity to the equation we'd been given by Mrs. Delphin (my first-grade teacher). But then, the most important step occurred—a step that solidified this simple equation as truth for the rest of our lives. We took what our parents said, what we learned in counting and addition, and we applied it to our own lives. Combing through what we had been told and our learning of all numbers, as well as our knowledge of the addition process, it became evident to us that two red apples plus another two red apples, equaled four red apples. This is how we truly learned the equation.

This is what learning from our pasts or our poor choices should look like. We all know someone who loves us who may have been through similar situations to ones we have faced or might be facing. The first step, just like in the "Red Apple" equation is going to them and just listening. Not for answers, but just to hear their situation, which choices they made, and what they would have done differently. In this sense, find your figurative "first grade teacher." This person should be someone you can confide in and vice versa. It should be someone you trust. The person is just there so you can see and hear another perspective. Let's continue learning.

Next, just like we had to dig deeper to learn numbers, how to count, and the addition process to further understand the equation, now in looking and learning from the past or the "What ifs," we must again dig deeper. Let's look at your situation and choices made in a deeper manner. Who were all the participants? How did it all begin? At which point during your situation did you choose your actions poorly? But more importantly, what emotion were you feeling at the time? It is important to note the emotion at this time because as we all know, when we act based solely upon our emotions often-times it leads us to undesirable outcomes. Frequently the dependence on emotional responses leads to the absence of reason or rationale. Therefore, singling out each emotion that led to a poor choice may prepare us to better control not only the emotion, but also the action elicited in response to the emotion.

Let us consider these questions while looking at a brief case study:

An argument between you and your sister erupts over the Christmas holidays. Some would say this is a very common occurrence amongst family members and usually occurs around the holidays. But why? Do we further examine why these things happen every year or after every family gathering? Since we can't control what anyone else does and we can only focus on ourselves, we will deal with these questions primarily based on "self." Let's begin.

Who were the participants? *You and your sister struck up a heated debate, which started over something trivial like which is better; Samsung or Apple. This simple debate ended with name-calling, feelings of hatred, and an overall lowering of what should be, "Happy Holiday" moments with the family. Well that is the beginning and the end, but it is important for us to examine the* middle, to better understand how we could have come to a less explosive result.

So, when did you make your decisions poorly? *You decided to escalate the debate when your sister made a joke during the conflict and some random person in the room laughed, making you feel belittled or like you were losing the argument. Remember, it was an argument that didn't really matter in the grand scheme of things.* **So what emotion or emotions were you feeling?** *You felt angry, you felt put down, and you felt attacked.* **How did you respond?** *You lashed out, insulting your sister and vowing to not join family festivities in the foreseeable future—all this over a conversation that was not important AT ALL.*

You see in this example that it would be possible to spend time pointing the finger or blame at the other party, using "What If" language for them, yet not using it on yourself.

For example, you might tell your sister, *"If you hadn't laughed at me and belittled my point of view, I wouldn't have made fun of your point of view and we wouldn't be in this situation."*

To which your sister could rebut, *"If you would just try to see other points of view instead of having to always be right, then we wouldn't argue every year."*

Notice, neither party here is looking inward. The truth is, we would be better served if we used the same "What if" language, but instead of directing it toward others, turned the tables and directed it toward self.

For example, you might think, *What if I had realized that the subject wasn't important enough to argue about? What if I had just agreed to disagree? What if I had been less worried about winning an argument and more focused on spending time with family?*

Would the results have been different?

After you have thoroughly dissected your "What if," things should seem a little clearer. This newfound clarity helps the next and final phase of Step 3. After digging deeper we have to now ask ourselves what we would do differently to elicit a better or more desirable outcome. Remember write it down and reread daily.

But wait; remember we haven't fully learned it yet until we apply it to our lives. This is why we must daily remind ourselves with our list of change so that when we are faced again with our difficult situations we choose the better action that will lead us to a better result.

We have done it. We are on our journey of learning from our "What if."

Step 4- As humans we will make mistakes. Some may be so drastic that we may feel that our lives have been ruined. At times, I've even looked into the sky and thought, *I'm done, and my poor decision has ruined my life*. But hopefully after steps 1-3 we have found a new outlook on our "What if" and we're ready to move forward.

Moving forward is definitely easier said than done. The reason for this is that moving forward requires a step that many people are reluctant to take because they feel they don't deserve it. Friends, that step is forgiveness. Not the forgiveness of another, but rather the utmost, heartfelt forgiveness of ourselves.

Think back. When was the last time someone forgave you after you truly apologized for any hurt or harm you may have caused them? Do you remember what it was like swallowing your pride and laying yourself at the altar of forgiveness in hopes that they'd see your sincere apology, accept it, and forgive you? Once they forgave you, think about how easy it was for the both of you to say, "Ok, we had a rough patch, you apologized, and I forgive you now let's move forward." This is the same with moving forward from mistakes we've made in the past. This process of moving forward will depend on us acknowledging in our hearts our wrong, promising to change, doing better, and then ultimately forgiving ourselves. With this forgiveness and moving forward, we have now reached a state of where we CAN have control, the "What is."

"Is" is defined as a state of living or existence; a present state of being. Remember, this chapter is dedicated to transferring our time, energy, and focus to the present and our current state of existence in order to forge a better present and future for our lives. That being said, let every day be the beginning of your life. Let's live.

So how do we live in the present in a way that allows us to reach our full potential and become all we were meant to become in this life? I encourage each of you to wake every day and ask yourself, "Will I thrive today?" "Will I give today all I have?" Wait…Pause… I mean literally wake daily and ask yourself these seemingly rhetorical questions, because like it or not, you will answer them one way or another; by your words or by your actions. We have no choice, because anything less will only lead to a life of regret and disappointment. Allow me to speak from my own personal experience.

I awoke one morning puzzled. I had graduated from college, no longer playing football, and taking my place in that dreaded "real world" as some would call it. Except this wasn't a reality TV show. It was my true reality. I began to look back mentally at all the good times that had passed as well as the difficult times. I must have spent about an hour just lying there pondering what great things I had done or the minor changes I would make if I could go back. Has this ever happened to you? "Those were the days" or "Boy I'm glad that's over."? We often look into our pasts in order to uncover those moments when we were happiest and also to look in retrospect at those moments that we are glad have passed. We've all been there, but now it's time to live in the present.

At times it seems as if the "good ole days" are gone, but part of living in the "What is" is making new "good ole days." Think about it. Think about the happiest time of your life. During that time, you never stopped and said, "Wow, I'm living the good ole days." This is why it's important for us to live in the NOW, accepting and enjoying life to the fullest. As stated earlier, we don't want to wake up years from now and see that we've done nothing with our lives and only lived in the past, spending years reminiscing about times that we can never get back. Instead, each of you should be striving to live a life that in five years from any moment you'll be able to say, "I wasn't perfect, but I have lived every moment for my "NOW," my WHAT IS."

While reading this chapter, I want each of you to remember this. We can dwell on our past mistakes throughout our entire lives on earth, or we can regain control of our lives and decide to learn from our pasts and live every day forward in the NOW, the present, the WHAT IS.

Which life will you choose to live?

GET OUT OF YOUR WAY

Why doesn't he want me to succeed? He robs me of every desire, while at the same time convincing me that complacency is fitting. I put him to bed every night that he may dream, yet he wakes daily only to crush those dreams of what I desire.

"You can do it, you are a great man," I say.

With great disdain he replies, "Well you're nothing, you're normal like all the rest."

It is only when I notice that I'm staring in the mirror that I see... that it is he... that is I; holding US back. I'm in my own way.

It is often found that our greatest adversary is the woman or man in the mirror. Just like it takes time for the light to bounce back and reveal who we really are when we're looking into a mirror, in life we can spend years wallowing in indecisiveness only to see that we are the culprits holding ourselves back. How many times have you woken up and inquired, "How did I get here in life?" Yet you lie down the same night telling yourself, "Tomorrow is the day I'll change and chase after my dreams. Tomorrow is the day that I'll go to the gym."

It is in this behavior that we must change our lackadaisical routine lifestyles, and stagnant situations. We must get out of our own way. Millions say, "It's in my heart to change, I just don't know how. I don't know where to start." So, let's figure out how; together let's search out a potential starting place.

We must first start by acknowledging the change we need to accomplish in our lives, whether that change is furthered education, financial stability, spiritual growth, learning to trust, bringing our families back together, or something as simple yet complex as learning to love ourselves. This list of changes could easily continue, but we'll let these goals suffice for now. However, I encourage you to look into that same mirror and ask yourself, "What changes am I holding myself back from accomplishing?" What new beginnings have you wanted to achieve for so long, yet you have been reluctant or afraid to take the first step toward them?

Now that we've laid out the "where to start" lets tackle the "how." First, with the help of author and Pastor Harry Simon Sr., I have prepared a prayer that embodies the strength and perseverance of the phoenix. It is a prayer that signifies that you too, just as the phoenix, will be able to look your hardships in the face and scream to it, "I WILL NOT BE MOVED, FOR I AM IMMOVABLE…UNBREAKABLE." Start by quoting the Prayer of the Phoenix while looking into your mirror of change.

"I WILL NO LONGER STAND ASIDE AND ALLOW YOU TO HINDER ME, BECAUSE I'M TOO STRONG, TOO BRAVE, AND UNSTOPPABLE, AND I REFUSE TO LOSE BECAUSE I WAS BORN TO WIN. THIS ROAD WON'T BE EASY BUT I CAN DO IT, I CAN CHANGE, I CAN LIVE AGAIN… I WILL WIN, I WILL WIN, I WILL WIN."

Though to some it may seem simplistic to perform this in front of a mirror, I recommend this because we need to see the strength we possess inside of us. We must feel the hairs on our necks rise as we declare our refusal to be stagnant any longer.

It is vital that the man or woman in the mirror has fair warning that the day of complacency is over, and that you are taking charge of your life. You are getting out of your own way!

The process has begun and there is no turning back now. We're on the right track. It's now time to walk through those doors we have been too fearful to venture through; time to crawl through those windows of opportunity that appeared to us and showed hope, though we refused to step out on our faith. Some may ask, "What if there are no open doors, or windows to change?"

Then recognize the change that needs to occur in your life, kick a hole in your situation, and walk directly through your new "self-made" entrance.

Make and form your own destiny and do not allow yourself to be denied. Remember, you're strong, you're brave, you're unstoppable…you can't lose.

This being said, being on the right path and being motivated are all great but remember we must build our house of change on a solid foundation or one turbulent wind of tests and anxiety will sway us. So, what's our solid foundation? Allow me to share a personal experience.

CHANGE:

I have so much to say, I want to give back to the world and help people. I want people to live, laugh, and love themselves. I want people to get out of their own way and accomplish all their hearts' desires. But why would anyone want to read what I have to say?

There will be people that say they've heard it all before and that this is just another self-help book. Who am I to give advice? Who am I to write a book?"

These were the thoughts that crossed my mind back in the summer circa 2010 when I knew I wanted to put my thoughts on paper and share them with the world. So, you see, people, we all face moments when our greatest adversary is staring us in the face, giving us every reason in the world not to chase after our dreams and conquer the world. However, it is in these times that our actions will determine if the cycle of blocking ourselves from reaching maximum potential is broken, and if we'll opt to kick holes in our situation and walk through our own figurative doors of opportunity.

In 2011, I walked up to the mirror, looked my greatest adversary in the eyes and said,

"I will no longer stand aside and allow you to hinder me because I'm too strong, too brave, and unstoppable, and I refuse to lose because I was born to win. This road won't be easy, but I can do it. I can change. I can live again…
I will win, I will win, I will win.

I was reciting the Prayer of the Phoenix. That very day, I picked up a pen, grabbed two sheets of paper, and began writing. I began making my change. I disregarded my anxiety and began the next seconds of my life with purpose toward the change I so desperately needed to make. In essence, I began to get out of my own way.

Now, I'd be remiss not to acknowledge that throughout the process there were times that I second-guessed myself and my efforts, but I just had to refocus and remember that

I was too strong to be broken or defeated by doubt and continue down my path of change. That said, I encourage each of you to start now. Sometimes, all that is needed for us to accomplish the dreams of our hearts is just simply get up, stop talking about doing something, and just do it. Keep in mind, there will always be naysayers. There will be those who doubt you, but remember the Prayer of the Phoenix. Your solid foundation begins when you take the change you need to make, figuratively mix it with the Prayer of the Phoenix, and then transform this into actions.

Be confident and excited at your new change because change in itself is contagious. There is a reason why the phrase, "Lead by example" is so widely known. Naturally, when you see someone doing something good it makes you want to be a better person. Think about the last time you saw an older gentleman holding a door open for his wife or pulling her chair out for her at dinner—didn't it just make your heart warm to know that such good deeds still exist in the world we live in today? This being said, stepping outside of our comfort zones and contributing positive change in our own personal lives will have spillover effect upon those who also want to change in a positive manner but just need that example set before them.

Wherever you are right now, I want you to stop reading and go take that first step toward your change and solid foundation. For me it was picking up the pen. For someone it might be taking a month off from partying with friends, and instead, investing that revenue into a nutritionist to increase lifestyle health. For another it might be as simple as finally setting "a date" for that lovely eleven year engagement you two love birds have been a part of. Whatever your desired change, let's take action. If your desired change is to bring your family closer together, stop reading right now, call your family, and tell them that you are changing and you love them. Tell them you will no longer live in complacent acceptance of how far apart your family has gotten.

Whether you've got a family rift to heal, or whether you've got personal, career, creative, or financial goals you're trying to meet, you are getting out of your own way. Whatever your first step may be, *stop reading now and go.* I'll be here waiting. No, I'm serious…this process can't work if you keep reading and skip this part. Though I am glad you are captivated, I am more excited about the change that is about to take place in your life. We will continue upon your return!

How do you feel? Some of us may have called family members, while others looked up a master's program in business. Someone sat down and wrote out a monthly budget to reach financial stability. I'm sure there's someone out there who said, "I'm tired of saying I only have fifteen more baby pounds to lose, even though my child is seventeen years old," so they went to the gym and began their change. Someone else looked his wife in the eyes and said, "Hey it's rough right now, but I love you and we are going to get through this. I made a commitment for better or for worse, so let's work together to make our marriage better." Then there is a forty-one-year-old single mother who sent the kids to Grandma's and pampered herself all weekend, because she deserved to feel loved by the person it means the most from; herself. You see, people, regardless of what change needs to occur in any of our lives, the first step is to focus on the Prayer of the Phoenix, realizing that there is strength within us, and then taking that strength and unbreakable attitude and transferring it into our actions. This is how we will get out of our own way.

Thank you all for starting your change.

Now, on our journeys of getting out of our own ways in order to create change there will inevitably be obstacles, anxiety, and failure. Let's deal with each.

THE OBSTACLE

An obstacle is defined as a person or a thing that stands in the way of or holds up progression. In a perfect world such a word wouldn't exist, but the reality is, while accomplishing our changes, we will undoubtedly face people or situations that will attempt to derail, hold us back, or get/remain in our way. Think of the principle of "crabs in a bucket." If you take one crab by the claw and begin to offer it liberation by pulling it out of the bucket of crabs, those below will clench on to him, making achieving his "freedom" that much harder. They want to pull him back down. We too will have those in our lives who see us trying to better our situation or lives and they will try to pull us down because they feel as though they are at the bottom of the bucket. They are our obstacle. Just like on an obstacle course, we must either go around, under, over, or through any obstacle in the way to get to the finish line. We must do the same with our obstacles in life, whether they are outside parties or situations that stand in the way of us accomplishing our dreams.

In getting out of our own ways and moving toward change we will also sometimes face failure. However, it isn't the failure that will decide our ultimate fate—rather it's our reaction or response to the failure that will not only determine our character, but also whether we'll remain in our own way or walk the path of change. People, failure in life is almost as natural as breathing. So, when failure comes, remember this; "Every present step is leading to the future." In your quest to get out of your own way, when you face failure, you must not stop, but rather remember your end goal and keep pressing forward. A wise man once said, "Imagining standing atop the mountain doesn't take away the fact that you still have to climb the mountain, but it does make that next step just a taaaaadddd bit more bearable."

If you are trying to accomplish financial stability, write a budget, quote the Prayer of the Phoenix daily, and begin living a life that allows for less financial strain. Don't be discouraged if one month you splurge and go over budget, because the fact is, time only stops for you when you leave this earth and wasting time getting down on yourself is futile. What is more fitting is to regroup, recognize where you went wrong, and just like in "What if vs. What is," forgive yourself through learning and future application. Then continue moving forward toward your financial stability.

Surely in our quest for change we will face anxiety. Anxiety is defined as fear of the unknown. This fear is not necessarily bad, because at times it is fear that will drive us forward in life pressing us toward our greatest potential. However, we often find ourselves fearful of the very thing that will make us happy. By this I mean that the risk we may face in order to reach our reward at times persuades us to sit in complacency in an effort to avoid potential failure or disappointment. This internal battle between risk versus reward affects every facet of our lives. For example, it may affect going for that promotion that you've wanted for so long, because you don't want to get your or your husband's hopes up. It might manifest as not asking your tenth grade crush out on a date until the last day of school before summer vacation, though you've been secretly in love with her all year. Or it might even mean finding the nerve to move to another country to follow your dreams of teaching English to non-native speakers, whilst furthering your passion for cultural studies. Within each of these examples, it is usually easier to sit in complacency rather than facing the potential of being told, "I'm sorry, you're just not quite qualified to run a sales team right now," or "Sorry Jason/Stacy, I don't see you in a boyfriend/girlfriend type of way. We are great friends though."

Easier to sit in complacency yes, but will that get you to your end goal? Will that allow you to become what your legacy demands? During these critical moments of choice, we have all heard our hearts figuratively beating outside of our chests and experienced the mental sweating of bullets, and increased body temperature. These expressions of anxiety can either lead us to complacency or propel us to get out of our own way.

I pose a question for those who are afraid of getting out of their own way. What are you more afraid of—risk associated with "Getting Out of Your Own Way" and taking control over your life, or lying down and getting up, ten, twenty, or thirty years from reading this very question only to see that you chose to do nothing but hinder your life? I'd only hope that the overwhelmingly majority of readers would have chosen to be more afraid of the latter.

Take every day with the Prayer of the Phoenix in mind and take daily steps toward accomplishing your change.

Get out of your own way!

I would even go so far as to recommend that this chapter be read weekly or monthly as a simple reminder to continue pressing through our greatest adversities in life.

I want to close this chapter with a little reflection. We have to remember first that this is a daily process. For in the moments where we fool ourselves into becoming complacent again, we will find ourselves missing out on life and all it has to offer.

Sitting in a doctor's office once, I witnessed an older lady ask a young man, "Sir, if you had the opportunity to move to the moon, would you take the chance?"

Simultaneously with the finishing of her question, the young man apparently began to think of all the negative reasons, which supported an answer of, "No ma'am, I wouldn't. My family is here, my money is here, I would have no place to live, and how long would it take to get there…?" etc.

Her reply was amazing. "Son, isn't it amazing how we so quickly think of reasons not to take or at least think about taking the opportunity of a lifetime, instead of allowing our minds to contemplate reasons to grasp these opportunities by the reins and ride off into the sunset? What if I told you the trip, with newer technology, was only a week long, all your family and friends could go, and because of the moon's special gasses, scientists have proven that a human's lifespan will automatically double."

He replied, "Well if you put it like that then my answer would probably be yes."

Sitting back and watching this conversation take place was the most inspiring thing for this chapter. What the woman ended the conversation with has changed my life ever since that day. She said, "Son remember, life is a compilation of choices we make, always, always, always keep an open mind when it comes to opportunities before we automatically jump to saying NO. Ask more questions, say yes more, and always keep your eyes open for an opportunity of a lifetime that could re-write your legacy."

In getting out of our own ways we must recognize that sometimes the opportunity of a lifetime knocks on our door and at other times it stands at the front door simply waiting to be invited in. Remember with our daily process toward change, to keep an open mind, search out your dreams, and constantly find reason to take those opportunities that may only appear once in a lifetime.

Get out of your own way.

DEFEAT,
HAVE YOU SEEN HER?

There she stood…boldly in front of me after lurking within the shadows of inevitability for what seemed an eternity. I knew she would find me, this day or the next. Unfortunately, my feeble attempts at a transparent existence had failed.

Did I really think I'd be rid of this thorn? This disappointment? This pain? Maybe not, but at the very least I'd thought I might possibly forego it just a little while longer. I wasn't ready to face the truth—to face the facts. I was merely torn from within as an internal conflict erupted. Though it may sound cliché, in this case I was losing both the battle and the war. I was her prisoner of war with very little hope for escape.

Unfortunately, my cell didn't consist of solitary confinement, maximum lockdown, or day to day barter for secured peace of mind. No…No, my imprisonment had been known by both myself and her, which seemed to be the world. My confinement consisted of the constant reminder that I'd lost and that I'd failed. Daily dragging my fetters of doubt throughout my seemingly indefinite term, had led to feelings of hopelessness. Had this state of surrender really become an option?

Define failure. Is it the nonexistence of an optimistic hope, or the acceptance of a current, undesired status in life for what it is?

Since life is so unexpected, we must have faith that failure is of the former. But who knows?

There's no fairy tale here, no pixie dust to assist in flight into a world where she didn't exist. Just here. Just now.

Uncontrollable eye contact between the two of us led to feelings of intense anger followed by a transformation to fear. Why was I afraid? Life would still go on after her.

Nonetheless, she smiled at me as though to symbolize her victory over me. On the outside I stood my ground, staring eye to eye without wavering and not showing or conceding that I had been emotionally and mentally affected. Inside though, yeah inside, I was crushed. This was the first time she'd affected me. As she turned away, I lowered my head to regain composure and some morsel of strength from within. I had to find this inner strength, since everyone expected a superman out of me, while not allowing me to have my own kryptonite. Looking back at her, eyes watering, blood boiling, and memories settling in ... all the "woulda, coulda, shouldas" came into play. She spoke with a smirk on her face—facetiously, as if we hadn't known each other . She reached out, touched me, and said sarcastically, "HI, I'M DEFEAT."

Stifled with silence, tongue seared to the roof of my mouth, I had no reply—no rebuttal full of wit, just concession ... I had to face her. It hurt. I was born to win, but not this day so it felt. This was the day the tides turned; my turn to learn gracefulness within humility. But simply put, it hurt. The pain cut through my heart like a hot scalpel through freshly whipped margarine. I greeted her knowing she'd be scrutinizing every facial expression and every breath with hopes of uncovering the severity of her metaphorical scars upon my human mind.

I had arrived. Here was my crossroad. Though it was not made of clay, gravel, or concrete; no, my crossroad was paved with choices that would affect me for the rest of my life. I was there—I'd arrived at my crossroad! Unbeknownst to me, the next moments would shape and define my character for years to come.

In the upcoming chapter, we are going to deal more in depth with this metaphor of facing defeat within our lives. Life is full of ups and downs, but also at times we are faced with decisions that can determine our fate for years to come. It is what we do at these moments that will either mark our legacy in the wet concrete of life or prove our character to be unworthy of obtaining the world and all it has to offer.

We all face our crossroads at some point. When you finally come to that crossroad and have to decide between turning around, giving up, and not feeling this pain anymore; as opposed to blindly pressing forward against the odds with no promise of victory, I want you to remember this: You may turn around, and granted, no longer will you feel your own individual pains, but be assured that that is the day you die. That is the day your legacy ends. However, if in that moment you decide to be courageous and press forward through your defeat, unknowing of an outcome or reward, I assure you, my friend, that's the day you'll live forever. All those who are remembered forever only accomplished this mental immortality because they too faced their crossroads, and chose to press forward. Though their roads weren't easy, and were often paved with turmoil, difficulty, mental and physical pain, and disappointments alike, we still speak of them today, because they persevered (Martin Luther King, John F. Kennedy, Gandhi).

It is because of these life-changing moments that we should not stray away from facing our crossroads of defeat, but rather we should relish the fact that though you are pressing forward with no promise of completion or victory, you are solidifying your place in life forever. Walk forward, my friends.

Let's deal with defeat.

I'M STILL BREATHING

So, what is life… besides the mere desire to survive, thrive, excel, and achieve? It's more; it is also pain, victory, defeat, and tests; all of which we live through daily. "We all must die, but very few of us actually live." This quote was one of the original motivations for this chapter; because it acknowledges the fact that our lives are finite, yet some choose to live it to the fullest while others just mosey through our vapor of an existence on this earth. Which will you be? Unfortunately for some, this isn't a decision that we can allow to just tarry until it disappears. This is because even if you are standing still, with time constantly moving forward, essentially you will always be moving backwards. Have you ever seen a building lay its own foundation? Was it possible for the masterpiece, The Creation of Adam, which coats the ceiling of the Sistine Chapel, to paint itself? How many orchestras have you heard that performed without a conductor? I pose these rhetorical questions because the fact is that in our lives we must take up our own journeys and lay our own foundations if we are to have any hope of reaching our full potential in life. We must pick up the paintbrush of persistence and daily paint our own masterpiece that it may be viewed not only as an example to the world, but also a constant reminder to ourselves that we won't be deterred from our destinies. And finally, in order to hear the beautiful harmonic chords of reward, we must not fear the inevitable in life but rather stand assured at the podium of our lives and conduct our symphonies in a way that pushes out tones of triumph.

Let's continue.

We're midway through our journey. So far, we've transferred our energy from the "What if" to the "What is." We've recited daily the Prayer of the Phoenix, and every day we're making a conscious effort to get out of our own ways while moving toward change. However, as we know, life isn't always as easy as reading a book or deciding to change and it happening. There will be speed bumps and at times we'll feel like we are on our last thread and won't make it to the next day. How many of us have been so close to throwing our hands up and giving up on life during these moments? When it seemed as though something as simple as fairness and justice had been given to everyone else but you? Times where it seemed that those who intentionally tried to cause you harm and at times succeeded, excelled while you kept getting the short end of the stick. It is because of these times that I encourage you to read this next quote carefully.

"Look how far you've come from the point you thought was the end."

I've tried to live my life during these crucial moments with the constant reminder that though this situation is tough and I can't see myself "getting out of this one," I've been there before, but *I'm still breathing*. Remember we control if defeat is temporary or if it becomes a permanent state of being; whether physically, mentally, or emotionally.

With Walt O'Malley's permission, allow me to paraphrase a story from his experience.

(June 2010)

"Today was one of those days. The kind where your heart wants to scream out into the dark abyss and ask for at least a glimpse of light. The day when you've done everything to the best of your ability to be on the side of right, yet the knock of fairness and comfort never approaches your door. I was broken; in every sense of the word. Gazing up into the rainy Texas sky looking for consolation, while reciprocating with my own raindrops, my mind begged for understanding while a million questions naturally circled my brain. How did I get here? Will my good deeds ever be accounted for? Will good ever overcome evil or is that just reserved for the fairy tales? Nonetheless, no answer ensued; just there, just then.

Allow me to provide some exposition. I identified June 2007- June 2008 as one of the most tumultuous years of my life. I found out that I was having a child before I was married and immediately I felt as though I had let everyone down. Feelings of, "What will people think of me now?" crept into my thoughts like a stealthy thief in the night. Nonetheless, I was raised to believe that every man must take responsibility for his actions and make the best out of every situation. So, for me, the course was simple; find a way out of no way and keep pressing forward. I had always been a guy who sided with prolife advocates, but it's always easier to stick with your beliefs when you aren't faced with large decisions that will alter the course of your life as you know it. For the first time in this respect, my beliefs were faced with reality and I was at a decision point. Though all thoughts of anxiety led to the fact that I had no earthly idea of how to be a father, I knew her life deserved a chance.

For weeks I fought off all mental debates that included what perception those closest to me would have, how I would raise a child in a world like this, or whether I should disregard my beliefs and think and act selfishly for the betterment of my life. This is when I thought back to the lessons from my younger years.

"Son, gold is never purged in a freezer, but rather it must be sent through the fire in very high temperatures in order to burn off all the impurities that halt it from being pure and precious. Embrace and outlast your fire and you will come out the other end as pure gold."

Because of these lessons, I made it through my decision point.

But this wasn't enough. I hadn't been purified yet. I found myself in a position that I would have never imagined in a million years. Turmoil began to creep in between my daughters's mother and me, and as a result, I found myself up many nights looking for answers that were never given. They say when it rains it pours. On the other hand, they sometimes omit that often with rain and winds come hurricanes and tropical storms. My situation quickly spiraled from bad to worse. Unimaginable situations became reality, unbelievable circumstances became actuality, and all reason and rationale became futile. A draining eighteen months of court dates; legal "sit-downs," in order for attorneys to get their "cut" off the top, led to feelings of defeat. Nonetheless, I pressed forward. Throughout it all I supported my daughter in every way imaginable and sacrificed all I had to ease any difficulties her mother would face, yet I found myself in front of a judge deciding if and how much I would be allowed to be in my seed's life. Deflated became the understatement of a lifetime. I was at the end of my rope.

Yet through all the inflicted suffering from outside parties, I tried to remain a good person, feeling as though my good deeds would be taken into account by a higher power—feeling that I'd hurt no more, and justice would finally find me. But it didn't.

On that day, I sat and watched a judge take something from me, and hand it to the inflicting party even though they had destroyed any hopes of peace for an entire year. My daughter was taken from me in every sense of the word and I was discarded as just another guy being abused by a flawed system. Now, I must clarify. It wasn't the fact that someone who had absolutely no idea of any of the events that had occurred for a year prior to the court date was making the final decision as to the fate of my daughter and me. Rather, it was about how my desire to do the right things and maintain the proper attitude even in the face of my inflicting enemies had no bearing on the decision. From birth we are pretty much raised being taught that good always overcomes evil; but on that day I couldn't see it happening. On that day, I felt as though I had lost. I felt defeated."

Have any of you ever felt like this? Has there been a time when all rationale points to getting even, or no longer turning the other cheek, yet you persevere in an upright manner, but at the end of the day you're still hung out to dry? If you've been here before then you understand the mental battles that take place at times such as these. However, remember friends, this too is a decision point, and if you recall, what we do in these critical moments will not only determine our character, but it will either imprint our legacy in the wet concrete of life or wash away our beautiful canvass of persistence.

Walt's story continued. *"I thought back to a time when I was in college. Coming from a lower income family yet trying to take my place in society with education, I found myself homeless. I couldn't make rent payments. I was parking at the on-campus housing parking lots at night, for safety, and sleeping in my vehicle; eating when I could find ninety-nine cents for a dollar-menu meal; while watching those around me live comfortable lives. I remembered that in those days I couldn't see my way out just like today. But there was one more commonality between June 2010 and those rough days in college; I was still breathing."*

"Life is tough, but without it you're dead."

This chapter is very special to me because it is what I hope those reading take from this book if nothing else. People, in any situation or hardship, and through all your tears and sleepless nights, if you are still breathing you have a chance.

In Walt's story, he gained strength throughout his tumultuous seas by reflecting on a previous moment in time at which he'd faced his potential demise. If you are holding on by a thread, I encourage you to tie a knot and hold on a little longer. Life may be tough and at times unfair, but if we began to realize that this is now, but *I'm still breathing,* then we will gain the strength to fight on. Even in pressing forward with no reward in sight, take solace in the fact that you have made a conscious effort not to be stagnant. Remember, defeat can be temporary or permanent, but only you can make that decision in your life.

Reflect upon this quote.

"Yesterday was tough, today was even more tough, but if it should come, I'll be better prepared for tomorrow."

By this I submit to you that every obstacle or hardship in your past as well as those to come are only preparing you for the rest of your tomorrows. Your tomorrows in which we will live on forever, planting our permanent tree of persistence on this earth that it may blossom as an example for all to see and follow. That's will power.

I want to pose a question. How much will power will you allow yourself to control in order to look your situation in the face and say, "You cannot kill me, I'm still breathing and I'm still fighting."

It is this will power that will allow us to accomplish anything, which will allow us to hurdle our personal thirty-foot walls in our lives. I am dedicating this chapter to the realization that whatever happens in life, we must focus on the fact that we are strong and that through persistence we'll continue living.

Think back to a time where you've thought, *This is what I've been waiting on.* You put all your energy into this basket, and it all came crashing down. Some may have even felt a sense of divine intervention leading them down the desired path.

(Side Note) Isn't it funny how "divine intervention" manages to always lead us down paths that we already desire, but never down paths that are probably less desirable yet more of a necessity in our lives? Just a thought!

Then suddenly, like an unpredicted mudslide, all your hopes and dreams are uprooted and thrown asunder. You're lost; torn to shreds even. The very thought of *How did I get here?* becomes futile because no answer ensues. It is in these times more than ever that we need to remind ourselves, "I'm still breathing." You still have a chance— a fighting chance.

I won't be as foolish as to think that in these times, emotionally and mentally lifting ourselves up is an easy task. But if in these times we realize that no matter how difficult our lives are at the moment, our hope is in the fact that we're still alive, this will sustain us through any peril that we all are sure to face at some point.

What does "I'm still breathing" look like? Let's personify this, and paint a mental picture.

MR. UNBREAKABLE

Picture this:

A man steps onto a cross-country course, preparing to run a race to the best of his ability. This mirrors life simply because all one can ask of any human in this race of life is to live a life to the best of his or her ability.

The man begins moving forward and with every step of the way, obstacles are thrown in his path. Have you ever felt that way? As soon as you make the decision to make a change in your life for the better, here come the obstacles? LOL, I heard a charismatic man say once, no girl ever wants me until I get into a committed relationship. A little comic relief... I digress.

The rain begins to pour, decreasing visibility, and he finds himself veering off course. The detour will not only cause his race to last even longer but now he's fighting the elements as his feet search for stable ground to no avail.

This, which began as just a simple race, has now become so difficult that thoughts of giving up creep into his mind. How many times have you taken the wrong path yet persevered thinking that your "never give up" attitude would push you through your detour, yet more and more obstacles were thrown your way? Would it be fair to say that in these times feelings of being overwhelmed and even thoughts of giving up seem almost allowable? But remember we are painting a mental picture of *I'm. still breathing.*

He fights off all thoughts of defeat because he wants to be a champion. He looks to the bleachers for support, but no one's there. No support, no one cheering. For all of you reading this, please understand that in this race, you won't always have someone backing your every move. Like a single mom raising a child on her own, there will be moments when you yearn for a shoulder to lean on or even for someone to share your excitement with, and yet all you'll have is *you*. If you're a father working three jobs to support your family, just as the runner, you must press forward because you too desire to be a champion.

Let's turn up the heat.

Imagine now that this man must run this race with a hundred resistant bungee cords strapped across his chest and remove them one by one while still running toward his finish line. However, to keep from being disqualified, he can't stop; instead he must remove the cords and press forward at the same time. His tasks seem impossible, unfair even. Have you ever felt this way? That you are waking up and going to work just like the next man or woman and yet your life is seemingly more difficult? Like every step forward you try to take, like these bungee resistance cords, something is always trying to pull you back?

Let's read on.

Nonetheless he wants to be a champion; he wants to be remembered for all eternity so he presses forward. Removing strap by strap, he's screaming in agony as his muscles buckle with exhaustion. He's fifty feet from the finish line and he's giving it all he has. Rain pouring, straps pulling him back, no support in the stands, and he's on his last leg (literally). He falls. "Stop, I've done more than others would have. This isn't fair. Why am I going through this?" These are the thoughts that consume his mind now that he has fallen. Often, we feel disappointed in ourselves during our temporary moments of defeat when these thoughts creep into our hearts. Understand that these thoughts are very natural, but it is how we act upon these thoughts that will prove to be far more important than the natural process of thought creation.

He contemplates his options and realizes, he's hurting, but HE'S STILL BREATHING. He's come too far. Champion that he is, he decides to fight on to the finish only to figure out upon standing that he's fallen into quicksand. How many times have we fallen and battled between the desire to give up or to do the right thing and press forward, only to get up and find ourselves in a worse place than before we even started the race?

He finds himself mentally broken, and he can't see his way out. He's come so far and now it's over. Have you ever felt this way? The feeling of, "I was already on my last thread, and now this?? I can't take anymore." What do you do? How do you respond?

He gives up… Slowly sinking to his figurative grave, he's disheartened. He fought with all his might and gave it all he had, and yet he was defeated. But remember that a champion, (which you are), even if he or she stumbles and fall, and can't see a way out, will never allow themselves to be defeated.

Immediately he thinks about how far he's come. Through rain, objects trying to hold him back, being side-tracked and taking the wrong course, with no support from anywhere, falling when so close to finishing, and he says to himself, "This isn't fair, this is tough, BUT I'M STILL BREATHING." He fights and kicks, treading the quicksand, yet steady sinking. But he doesn't give up because he knows everything that happened in this race was for a reason. Keep that in mind when you're in your quicksand of life. There is a reason, so always keep fighting.

"Kicking and screaming, "I won't be denied, I won't be denied, I'M STILL BREATHING," he reaches out and his fingers clench a nearby vine. He slowly begins pulling himself out, and then suddenly the vine snaps. Still fighting, he finds vine after vine after vine until he finds the one that is strong enough and long enough to pull him out. When he thinks all hope is lost, he gets out. He has fought his way through. Limping to the finish line, soaked by rain, covered in mud, cut, bleeding, and bruised up by the straps, he crosses the finish line.*

With tears in his eyes he beats his chest, and turns around to his race. He looks his situation right in the face and screams with the voice of war angels, "I can't lose, because I was born to win. I'M STILL BREATHING."

Friends, this is the epitome of what I want you to take from this chapter. This figurative race that he ran was probably the most difficult he'd ever run. Just like in our lives, every step forward he took, another obstacle was placed in his way. What he didn't realize as we often don't, is that by veering off track and getting lost, he was forced to think quickly to find his way back to where he was supposed to be. When the rain began to pour, he was forced to take sure, solid steps with perfect form in order to keep from falling.

This parallels our lives because it is in the moments when everything is going wrong that we most need to take sure steps.

It is in the moments in our lives when we veer off course that we need to look in depth at how we got where we are and quickly get back on track. When the straps were pulling him back with resistance, as we often have things and people in our lives trying to hold us back from success, his muscles grew stronger and stronger with each and every step forward. So even though it won't always feel good knowing that your friends, your enemies, your family, or different situations, may tend to try to keep you from your own finish line, be assured my friends that these obstacles are only making you stronger. Just as the figurative man in this race, take sure steps one by one, and remove each strap in your life that is trying to keep you from reaching your full potential.

*"One sure step forward sets you on the right path,
because whether right or wrong, learning begins."*

When he had no support in the stands he taught himself to be his biggest fan and press forward. This reflects our lives because often when we have a dream or a desire, the only person that will be in your corner is the person you see in the mirror. So just like the man in the race, make sure you are always your biggest fan. When he fell in quicksand, he saw firsthand what it was like to constantly do the right thing, and yet hardships befall you. This was the climax of his race because unknown to him he was at his decision point; his crossroad. He had reached the point where he would either give up or say to his hardship, "I'm still breathing" and fight on. He fought and he won.

Remember our quote; "Yesterday was tough, today was even more tough, but if it should come, I'll be better prepared for tomorrow." Unknowingly through this race and the obstacles our runner built endurance, physical strength, mental agility, will power, and a keen sense of focus, but most of all the recognition that regardless of what peril attacked him, he was still breathing. So, I ask you, "Is he better prepared for his next race?"

How does this metaphor apply to you?

Now that we've painted the picture of what "I'm still breathing" looks like, now we must apply it to our lives. Remember just like the man in the race, we do not know what always lies ahead for us. In each step we take, we must plant ourselves in solid ground throughout our race of life, so we'll remain upright. The rains are sure to come, the winds of change are sure to howl throughout our individual races, but persevering through all conditions is what gets us across that finish line in life.

Think about your own situations. In the times you feel like everything is trying to pull or hold you back like the resistance bungee cords, you must press forward one step at a time because this will build your strength.

For Walt, it took consistent effort at working through ideas, thoughts, and emotions with his daughter's mother. When I was speaking to him again years later prior to my publishing this book, Walt shared, *"I'm not saying that things are perfect, but we are one step closer to the finish line. (She may not agree, lol.)"*

When it feels like nobody is there to support you, press forward, my friends because you are still breathing and you are learning to be your own biggest fan, which is priceless. You may take the wrong path in life from time to time, but just like the man in the race, at that moment it is not fit for you to sulk in your bad decision but rather realize that you are still in the race to becoming a champion, find your way back on the right path, and keep pressing forward. When you reach your lowest point, which we all inevitably will at some point in life; the point where you can't see yourself "getting out of this one," kick, scream, fight, *don't be denied.* It is ironic that in the final moments of the race, the man pulled each vine to save himself, and yet each snapped and provided zero relief. He kept searching. This is what we must do in life as we begin to pull ourselves out of peril. Fight until the end and pull yourself out of your quicksand of life.

I don't care if you have to crawl across the finish line. At all costs you must make it. Looking back over your life and seeing that your entire life and the many barriers it handed you have led you to this point, you have come too far to turn around.

When you cross that finish line, thinking about how much stronger, faster, and smarter you are, turn to your situations in life, beat upon your chest, and scream, "I'm still breathing!"

You've made it my friends. Live on!

NO REGRETS

"If today was your last day on Earth, what would you do, where would you want to go, who would you call?" We've all come across these questions at some point in time in our lives. What's funny, is that often-times the answers we render are somewhat extreme, unbelievable, and some would even deem absurd. But why? Who decides what's unbelievable or extreme? What force of nature determines the unbelievable from the believable? It's sad to think that we go through this life only allowing our minds to fully exercise their imaginations after the hypothetical, "last day on earth" position is imposed upon us. Before some of you get ahead of yourselves and think that this chapter is dedicated to bungee jumping, reckless lifestyles, or bucket-list fancies, please allow me to shed some light. This chapter is solely dedicated to pulling back the scab of "going through the motions in life," that we may bleed a more fulfilling life of happiness. I'm talking about a life where we accomplish the unbelievable, and one where we face our fears and chase after our hearts' dreams. It's a life where we don't wait until the end wishing we had travelled there, or told him "I love you," or asked her, "Will you marry me?." In short, I'm talking about living a life with no regrets.

Robert F. Kennedy once said, "Some see things as they are and ask why. I dream things that never were and ask why not." This belief that anything and all dreams are possible can only come alive with the breath of desire and persistence blown into each of our lives.

Presented to me on December 27th 2007 by Christopher Thurmond, this quote imprinted three demands on my life.

1. To be optimistic in hope.
2. To expect greatness.
3. To make things happen.

Let's deal with each.

Optimism is defined as a tendency to expect the best possible outcome, but hope is defined as the cherishing of a desire with intense anticipation. In order for us to begin living life without regrets, we must first anticipate our desires to be possible with the confidence that we will achieve them.

Expecting is defined as the act of looking forward to the probable occurrence or appearance of a certain thing or object. In this I ask—what would define greatness for you? I implore you to look past finite and feeble monetary items, and really ask yourself, "What would make me great?" We must begin this process by ignoring the nay-sayers and as Kennedy points out, live life with the expectation of your individual greatness. Kennedy bought into the idea of living life with the thought that greatness can not only be achieved but also that we should wake every day, evaluate our potential, and fight to reach and surpass it.

The third pillar is the piece to the puzzle that separates the talkers from the champions. If you take nothing else from this chapter, I encourage you to remember this: Our imaginations are only confined by the barriers and medians of our minds. Remember there was once a time when cars did not exist, a time when the "world-wide web" was only at best, a spoof of the classic movie, *Charlotte's Web*. What I'm trying to say is at every turning point in humanity's journey, someone had to step outside the status quo and allow the unthinkable to become the "OMG, how did we ever live without this?" For this reason, the principle of making things happen must begin with thinking past current realities, and making your imagination reality. Some may say that accepting and taking some of these risks to better and change our lives is much easier said than done. This is true. However, it is important to understand that I am not encouraging everyone reading to begin taking nosedives into every desire and every craven thought they've ever had. Instead, I'm simply advocating for the proper amount of calculated risk to be mixed with passion and desire to help us live with no regrets. When these three steps become a part of our daily lives how can one have regrets?

Let's Transition.

In our daily lives, fear is often disguised as caution. In its noun form, caution is defined as carefulness or a warning. Now, we must all maintain a level of carefulness throughout our journeys, but we must daily evaluate this caution that we don't fall into the trap of allowing fear to be disguised as caution. Unlike caution, ill placed and/or poorly managed fear has the potential to deter us from living a life of fulfillment. Though I'm not talking, spiders, snakes, sleeping in the darkness, or other common phobias, I'm talking about the fear of stepping outside our comfort zones to achieve those feats that our hearts desire yet from which fear blocks us. In this case, fear becomes our invisible barrier to our destinies in life; our personal imagination-confinement chambers.

Let us now discuss comfort zones.

Comfort is defined as a state of ease and satisfaction or a person or thing giving consolation. A zone is defined as a predesignated location or area. By these definitions, our comfort zones in life are simply predesignated areas that are easy and satisfying to us, which provide some level of comfort or familiarity.

Ground-breaking I know… Just stay with me for a second!

In many modern-day, smoke-free airports, it's often found that not only can people not smoke freely outside the building, but if they choose to smoke they must stand in a predesignated area; which is often marked off by a bolded green line painted on the ground. In an effort to protect the air quality and breathing health of the majority at these airports, smoking outside of this area is forbidden and punishable by a fine. When we stay in our comfort zones for five, ten, fifteen years in life, we figuratively mirror the unfortunate souls forced to stand in our own figurative ten by ten-foot green squares, instead of inhabiting all life has to offer. Figuratively speaking, if these people remain in this predetermined zone for five years, their lives, just like ours if we remain in our comfort zones, will have been a waste. This is not to say that being comfortable is a bad thing, but rather that being permanently complacent in comfort will only make for unproductive lives and lifelong feelings of regret.

(Side note) The Chamber

I came back to edit this chapter approximately four years after writing it. To my surprise and dismay, the airports had evolved. The very smoking sections that were predesignated for outside use only, were now inside the busiest airport in the world, Atlanta

Hartsfield Jackson…Yes, "smoking rooms within terminals." I got quite a kick out of this as I wondered how in the world I would edit this portion of the book to include these new findings. Chuckling because it had taken a total of four years for progression in this sense to occur, I thought, "Maybe it's a good thing we didn't publish the book before seeing this advancement." By advancement, I meant this evolution to an indoor smoking room, which allows its patrons to partake in a puff within the airport without leaving the terminal.

Would this contradict my theory of marginal progress to be had within comfort zones? After thinking it through, I realized that it wouldn't. This progress was a good thing for smokers worldwide, but it had taken approximately four years to come to fruition. That said, we have all seen progress when operating within our comfort zones, but the question we should be asking is, "Are we willing to wait years for such minimal progress to occur?"

Upon seeing this new, air-filtered "Test & Learn smoke room" in Atlanta, I remember sitting across from it and just watching for a moment. The sliding door would open and close, allowing patrons in and out at their will. I watched carefully and was astonished at how the engineers had created a filtration system that only allowed minimal smoke to be released to the "General Public"; a true win for smokers all around the world. I waited, watched, and wondered…."What kind of revelation or meaning can come out of this?" Then it hit. The door continued to open and patrons continued to fill the room. The more smokers who entered, naturally, the more smoke filled the room, so much so that it became cloudy and visibility decreased more and more.

There it was. For those cold winter afternoons, having a location within the terminal to smoke was definitely progress, however, this progress was only as good as the current advances in smoke-room engineering and/or the ratio of smokers juxta-posed against the desire for visibility whilst smoking. As a point of clarity, I have nothing personally against smokers, however, I see a comparison to our lives when we find ourselves within our comfort zones and make it a point to remain. The longer we stay within our comfort zones, forgoing strides toward personal, mental, financial, spiritual, physical, or whatever growth mandatory for your flight toward excellence, the visibility outside our glass doors of life decreases. This inevitably leads to an eventual life of "cloudy" regret.

Remember, we were born to live with no regrets. This being said, we must constantly reevaluate our levels of comfort, while increasing our hunger for getting more out of life. If you work for a company, then start thinking of how you can perform better at your current duties, which will set you up for upward mobility. Keep in mind that moving upward is not limited to financial growth, but it also includes personal goals met, recognition received for jobs well done, inspiring others through your work ethic, and changing someone's life through your dedication to your craft, occupation, or career. If you are unhappy with your health, whether it's your weight, blood pressure, eating habits, or simply the aging of your body leading to complications, I ask you this, "Are you going to sit there and just take it in regret, or are you going to do something about it?"

You see, it's easy to not like things about our different stations in life, but it's important to remember that the mere disgust with where we are in life changes nothing. If we so choose, laying the foundation bricks of transformation throughout our journeys can be so beautiful. Planting the seed of determination in our lives, watering it daily with strategic actions, and watching it blossom into a rose of "no regrets" is definitely a beautiful thing. I encourage you to not go another moment in complacent comfort, but rather step outside of your own personal green bolded lines and inhabit better health.

No regrets!

Contact a nutritionist, who specializes in better consumption habits, to gain better tips on a healthier lifestyle and essential "know how." Join a gym that you may no longer live in regret for your current state. Granted, unless we have a time machine we can't do anything about, "how we got here," but we can get out of our comfort zones and inhabit all life has to offer now! Are you willing to live without regrets? On a side note, living a long life and aging is a beautiful thing, and it doesn't have to be something that we dread. If we strive for perfection in whatever point in life we are in, it is impossible to have regrets.

For example, a baby can't run a marathon, but babies are perfect in their state when they are just learning to crawl and taking their first steps. By this I speak to aging. Love yourself, eat healthy, work out, and live a life of total fulfillment, and regret will be impossible. Be perfect in your state.

Throughout this journey of no regrets, some may say, "Well, there is already a lot that I regret that I can't change." To that I say, the best time to plant a tree is twenty years ago, but the next best time to plant a tree is right now. This quote sums up the importance of realizing that we can't change the past but we can learn from it and live in the present, and therefore forge a better future. Remember, we have already transferred our energy from the "What if" to the "What is" and we are making a conscious effort to get out of our own way, which includes not harping on the uncontrollable past, and moving forward to live with no regrets.

You can do it! We can do it!

I want to share a brief story. It was the summer of 2004 in Houston, Texas and I was just going about my daily routine. I had just finished football practice and a couple of the guys and I were heading home but we decided to stop and pick up a quick meal from a fast food restaurant. In the car, joking around, we found ourselves laughing so hard that most of us had some form of precipitation coming from our eyes. For the life of me I can't remember what we were joking about at the time, but just recollecting the emotions almost makes me laugh now. I'm talking about the kind of laughter that they say is good for the soul. You know the kind where your abdominal section begs you to stop under penalty of convulsions and cramping. Yeah, it was that kind of laughter. Anyway, as we were riding along, we pulled up to a red light, and I happened to look out of my window and saw a young lady in the car with a young man. They both were crying hysterically as though they had just lost someone who was dear to them. Tears were streaming down my face due to laughter, and tears were streaming down their faces due to some form of pain. I couldn't imagine what they were weeping over—I could only equate it to the feeling I'd feel if I lost my father or when I lost my grandfather. My heart wanted to reach out to them and provide some form of consolation, but I couldn't.

This situation stood out to me. Here I was in one of the happiest times of my life and someone at a stoplight less than ten feet away from me was probably at one of their lowest moments in life. Because it is inevitable in life that we will experience both highs and lows, it is important to cherish, enjoy, and learn from the "highs" in life, that we may become stronger to persevere through the "lows" that visit us from time to time. That being said, if you have regrets already, remember that it is impossible for the rain to last forever and that after every storm the sun eventually comes out again and kisses the hairs on your head. Soon it will peak over the horizon of turmoil and scorch the salted tears from your cheeks, reminding you that you are still here and still have a fighting chance. Sometimes we just have to release the storms of regret and take solace in the calm we currently reside in. The present is now, it's here, and it's time to start living. Take a step.

Phase 1-Imagination

Before we wrap up this chapter, I want to shed some light on the spectrum of living with no regrets. Earlier, I spoke of imagination. It is vital to remember that we must not confine our imaginations to things that have been done, but we should allow our minds to think beyond the impossible. Why can't you own your own company? Why can't you be the one to find a cure to HIV? Why can't you be the one to work with government relief programs, aiding millions worldwide? Why can't you be the one who pulls your torn family back together? That's just it. You can! The most important phase in living with no regrets is first allowing your mind to imagine the impossible and the fact that "impossible," when separated, is "Im-possible." Because you are possible, impossible no longer will exist in your life. From the creation of the telephone, the invention of the first motor vehicle, and the harvesting of electricity, to the idea of equal rights for all mankind; each of the formulators of these ideas had to realize that impossible could be triumphed over by "Im-possible."

Are you willing to believe? This is true imagination, friends.

In the face of all adversity you must embrace the fact that "Im-possible" can only outweigh impossible if you set your imagination free. Let her, your imagination, soar high like the phoenix. *That's what she was meant to do.*

Though there has been controversy for decades over who created the telephone, I want to shed light on both Alexander Graham Bell, and Elisha Gray. Both imagined a world where communication was not limited to face to face conversations or week-long messaging. Before these two ambitious inventors came along, communication was restricted to basic mail delivery and telegraph. I pose this question—have any of you ever received a telegraph? It's funny to think how the imaginations of two people changed and shaped the entire world as we know it.

We all know Steve Jobs, but would Steve have been able to give one of the most amazing speeches of all times, "The New Is You," or shape the world of connective technology, if these imagination visionaries hadn't come before him? This is true imagination. I dare each of you to sit and watch TV for an hour on a mainstream station and not see some type of telephone provider commercial; all because two people who believed in the concept of "Im-possible". Consider this: In a hundred years, who will be writing a book thanking you for your contribution to this earth?

Phase 2-Application

As we all know, living a life with no regrets doesn't stop at imagination. As Kennedy pointed out, we must make things happen. This phase is important because it's easy to talk about changing your life, but when it's time to take that first step, look to your left and then your right and see if those enthusiastic talkers are by your side then. Often, this is not the flashiest phase, but without applying imagination with a process to bring it to reality it will never blossom, but will wither and die.

Karl Frierich Benz, generally regarded as the originator of the gasoline-powered automobile, imagined a world of faster and more efficient travel. To be able to maneuver through a town, between states, or even countries at rapid speeds at this time was seen only as a visionary's outrageous thoughts. But Benz took his thoughts and changed our world.

Without giving the entire history of the gasoline-powered vehicle, I want to shed some light on Benz's transition from the imagination phase to the application phase. As a child, Benz faced adversity, losing his father at a young age. Nonetheless, he progressed through his education and later studied mechanical engineering at the University of Karlsruhe. What's even more spectacular, is that he was accepted when he was nine years old and graduated at ten. At a young age, Benz bought into the fact that impossible could be outweighed by "Im-possible." Some would see this as the accomplishment of a lifetime, but we must keep in mind that application itself will spur more imagination. I want to say that again.

Application itself will spur more imagination.

Benz wanted more. Loving his bicycle from a young age, he imagined a motor carriage; one that would provide safe and fast travel independent of an animal. He took his imagination and ran with it. Benz went from creating factory engines for steel mills and iron workshops, to creating and obtaining patents for multiple of the essential parts to the modern-day vehicle. For example: the ignition system that used sparks with the battery, spark plugs, gear shifts, the clutch, speed regulators, and the radiator. To gain more revenue to change his imagination into reality, he applied his skills in a bicycle repair shop, which later began the production of gas engines.

You see, even Benz at times had to take a step back from his dreams and make the means to accomplish his dreams. This is important because we have all, at some point, had to sacrifice what we wanted most in life for a moment in order to have the ability to obtain it at its proper time and in its entirety. But it is vital not to see this temporary sacrifice as failure but as triumph of mind over matter. In these cases, we have disciplined ourselves to stay the course and ultimately gain a higher sense of appreciation for our future accomplishments. This is a pure example of sacrificing now for a better future, and I want to deal with this more in depth, but for now let's continue.

With his revenue and experience, Benz transitioned from imagination to application by using his prior creation, the gas engine, as well as the concept of the bicycle to create the first automobile. He received his patent on January 29th 1886.

Just like in our lives, Benz faced much adversity while seeking his gasoline-powered automobile. The application phase in our lives won't always be smooth but the key is imagining past the impossible and taking the first steps toward applying your imagination in hopes of bridging the gap between impossible and reality. Once you have an idea, investigate what it will take to accomplish your dream, and from that day forward think and act strategically in order to transition your dream from imagination to reality. Go, step out there on a limb, and change the world as we know it. Remember, what will be written of your contribution in years to come?

Phase 3- Persistence

As we sum up living life with no regrets, this phase is very important as it is often the toughest to master: persistence.

Persistence is defined as insistently repetitive, or continuous in effort or thought; existing for a long or longer than usual time. In its verb form, it is defined as being stubborn or diligent, primarily throughout obstacles. I want to make sure we are all on the same page, as this is the most crucial phase to living with no regrets. It is very easy to be persistent when everything is going great. Working toward a dream when your bank account is full, when you have the support of your family, and when the entire world is screaming your name and on your team, definitely makes persistence much more attractive. But I pose this question—how is your persistence when faced with adversity? How much do you persist when door after door is slammed in your face? When everyone around you excels, yet you're left in the dust? This, my friends, is the true test of character. My goal for you in reading this phase is to understand that throughout our individual quests to transition from imagination to reality, there will be times when we have done everything under the sun, correctly and properly, yet for some reason or another, we fall short of our dreams. Doors are closed in our faces; opportunities are given to those who appear to not really want it as badly as we do. But remember, in order to live without regret we must persist.

When our backs are against the wall, bill collectors are calling daily or there are unexpected pregnancies or declining economic and financial statuses, and the feeling of barely hanging on by a thread creeps in, how do we respond? We must remember that once again, we have reached our cross-roads and our next few choices will shape our characters for years to come. So, in these times, though racing forward may appear impossible, take a step, then take another, and another and before you know it, you'll look back and realize the strength you possess, and you'll see how far you persisted in the face of adversity. After doing so, your individual jour-neys will be completed and you will be remembered among the pantheon of all the greats who changed our world as we know it.

Equal Rights for All Mankind

I have chosen this example because this imagining was once seen as impossible, but through the persistence of those who saw it as "Im-possible," humanity has made large strides toward making this a reality. The amazing thing about persistence is, just like the fight for equal rights, persistence is a daily battle. We must never become complacent in the strides we've made or we'll never reach the end goal. Daily on our journeys we must run through walls of nay-sayers, jump over barriers of impossibilities, and fight through winds of resistance.

We can do it. We will do it.

Women not being able to vote, African enslavement, Jim Crow laws, Chinese labor camps, Japanese WW2 impris-onment camps, The Holocaust, South African genocide, oppressive dictatorships, and The Trail of Tears, are just a few examples of the horrors and inequalities innocents have suffered at the hands of humanity. Though many of these atrocious acts are behind us, inequalities still exist in today's societies. Because of this fact, we must take pride in the victories and strides we've made, but persist in completing the cause, which in this case, is equality for all. These examples, clearly point to the fact that persistence is not a one-time deal, but something that we will have to work at daily. Smile at the progress, but remember we have a lot more to accomplish. Regardless of what your own personal challenge may be, keep in mind that living with no regrets begins with allowing your imagination to breathe and live, then transitioning that imagination to the application process, fighting every day to persist when you are surely faced with adversity. Just like John F. Kennedy believed Americans and all mankind alike should be equal, we must also take a stand for our dreams, apply our actions to reach our goal, and then persist through our challenges. Doing this will allow us to solidify our legacy just as Kennedy has been solidified.

Figuratively speaking, true persistence in a dream means that regardless of the challenge, we must be willing to die for what we believe in. Remember, those who fight through barriers and press forward, shape the world. I want to be a Nelson Mandela, a W.E. B. Dubois, an Elisha Gray, or a John Locke. But more importantly, years from now I want someone to say, "I want to be persistent like Harry Pierre Simon."

What will they say of you?

In conclusion, we were made to live without regrets. We can accomplish this by stepping outside of our comfort zones and allowing our minds to think outside the status quo to reach a new reality. Combine the equation of Imagination + Application + Persistence and it will render a sum of Im-possible. Impossible will no longer exist.

Live with no regrets, my friends.

3, 2, 1, 0

Ever since the beginning of time, the end has been inevitable. Whether we fight it, deny it, or forcefully comply with this fact, it comes nonetheless. However, I pose these questions. How will you be remembered? What marks will you leave on this planet, and what will people say of your character for generations to come? In every aspect of our lives, the clocks will always run down to zero. The only thing we can control is how we choose to spend each lifelong ticking of our clock; which in turn engraves our legacy amidst the wet concrete of life. It is because of this inevitability of life that I'll dedicate this chapter to living every second, hour, and day to the fullest, and in doing so we will leave behind a trail of victory, persistence, and success.

Throughout this journey, I encourage you to open your hearts and look in retrospect at your lives thus far, that you may see how you've lived, and in turn see how you will begin living. Let today be the beginning of our lives! I want to share two brief stories.

German Oasis

I travelled to Europe in the summer of 2006. After landing in beautiful Munich, Germany, I later took a train to Prague, Czech Republic. This was a land full of beauty and rich culture, which I encourage each of you to visit one day. It's one of the few European countries still preserved with castles, cobblestone roads, grand cathedrals, and fields upon fields of non-Westernized open air.

During this train ride I gazed out the window and witnessed the inspiration for this chapter. In an old German country town by the name of Dusseldorf, lay an old house in the middle of a field. Now make no mistake, this wasn't your Western society average, four-bedroom, three and a half-bathroom family home. No. This house was a rust-colored, barn-styled home surrounded by tall grass with a pond out front. There was a birdhouse style mailbox, with wind chimes made of what appeared to be carved-out bamboo limbs, swaying ever so gently in the cool summer breeze. Like something out of a Robert Frost poem stood a very large oak tree perfectly positioned near the pond with a rope long and large enough to catapult any daring soul into the cold, still pond water. Yes, I know, sounds more like a countryside oasis than a normal place of residence. Tall grass blew in the wind and fresh air filled my lungs as we passed by. I kind of smiled inside as it brought me a sense of peace since this was my first time in Europe. Then out of nowhere, two little kids, one boy, one girl, and their little dog came running through the field in utter enjoyment—no PlayStation in hand, no handheld gaming device, not even an iPhone to download the latest app that taught "how to run gracefully in a field." Nope—just them, their dog, and the open field. If you can imagine the pure joy on their faces you'd swear they'd found their very own utopia and decided to live there forever.

This struck me because here I was on my way to study abroad in my serious world, focused on bettering my future and taking my place in society; both of which are essential.

But seeing this reminded me that at some point I needed to step back and enjoy this finite life for what it is.

People, there are only a few things in this life that are definite. Because we know that our lives are finite, we must live each day to the fullest. Just like the children frolicking through the field, it is for us to embrace this earth and enjoy every ticking second of our time on it.

I want to deal with this in depth but first allow me to share another brief story.

Mile-High Pinball

Aboard a flight to Texas to visit my family, I found myself writing one of the previous chapters, only gazing up to thank the stewardess for making me a drink as well as for an occasional session of people watching. Since I was flying from San Francisco, California, the people-watching sessions were definitely interesting and not a hair shy of entertaining to say the least. Nonetheless, I witnessed an event that would totally change not only this book, but my thought process on "3, 2, 1, 0" all together.

I'd purchased my ticket late, so I found myself sitting in a middle seat as well as directly over the engines and wings. As I'm sure you probably know, this is the loudest place to sit on the plane but also the worst place to be sitting if you are trying to concentrate and write a book. Midway through the flight, a young lady from about eight rows forward exited her row and proceeded to the back lavatory. I noticed her, but really didn't pay too much attention to her as she proceeded down the aisle. Then suddenly, as though she had become light-headed, she began to stumble and eventually pin-balled from row to row and later ended up on the aircraft's floor. You could hear the gasps of concern emitting from all those that had witnessed it firsthand. Fortunately, there was a physician on the plane who rushed to her aid. Turns out the young lady hadn't had any water, food, or rest that day due to travels, and she'd just gotten lightheaded from standing up so fast. Everyone on the plane was relieved, yet this situation stood out to me.

Here was this woman, making a routine trip to the lavatory, as we so often mosey through our lives habitually, yet she'd managed to gather the attention of almost the entire plane.

Friends, when we find ourselves living in complacency, succeeding, failing, or just going through everyday life, often our actions will have spillover effect on many people around us. The question then is, "What kind of effect will you have on those around you?"

These are two totally unrelated stories, but both are essential to understanding the concept of "3, 2, 1, 0." Allow me to shed some light on each.

German Oasis

This story screams out to humanity, "Live in the moment while enjoying every second." Though the primary message is quite simple, despite the fact that these kids, according to societal measures of wealth, were on the lower end of the totem pole, they exemplified the true epitome of being thankful for what you have and loving life for what it is. This is not to say that desiring or the acquisition of material things on this earth is vile, but it is simply to introduce the idea of loving what you have, while bettering yourself and your status, but at the same time stepping back at times and enjoying the now for the now. When was the last time you pulled to the side of the road simply to admire the flowers, sat on a porch at dawn simply to witness the splendor of earth's sunset, or spent an entire day smiling and being cheerful with each person you crossed, simply to bring your contagious happiness to others?

A wise man once quoted to me, "You've never seen a U-Haul behind a hearse!" Though I'm sure we have all heard this at some point or another, the concept still applies. The fact is, regardless of what we acquire on this earth, to my knowledge we cannot take it with us when we make our "grand exits." Many know; the Egyptians tried it by stocking their pyramids and graves with jewels, golden statues, and vast fortunes, and it didn't go too well. Therefore, I encourage all of you to at times run through your own metaphoric fields of joy, let down your hair, and enjoy the now for now!

Mile-High Pinball

This story too is vital to living our lives conscious of the ticking of our clocks. Live, people, live, but what is life if lived without a positive-influence trail left behind? Think about it—how many people do we have the opportunity to affect daily? If everyone lived with the thought of positively affecting those around them, how much better would this world be?

I encourage each of you to start within your own homes. For the next week, each of you sit down with your families, friends, or those closest to you and establish that you all desire to affect each other in a positive manner, and then watch the power of living life with "3, 2, 1, 0" in mind. All we have to do is turn on the news and we will see that there is enough negative going on in the world. Keeping in mind that our actions will always affect others, we should live our lives with the desire of positively affecting those around us.

"3,2,1,0....."

Now here is the irony of "The mile-high pinball." Because I found myself writing at the time of the airplane incident, my mind immediately tried to find meaning in the events that occurred. My row-mate Jake Sloss leaned over and said, "I'm glad she got back up and was ok." I told him that he had no clue how much that one sentence affected me that night. It's because of his unknowing wisdom that it all became evident to me. Sometimes in our daily lives we're going to fall, and bad things will happen for no apparent reason at all. We will also find ourselves in situations that are one hundred percent not our faults. It is in these times that we must not look for some nonexistent, futile reasoning, but just get back up and keep walking down our paths. Remember, our lives are finite, so our "3, 2, 1, 0s" are way too short to spend useless time on our figuratively mile-high floors trying to figure out the whys.

No, my friends, I encourage you in these times to slowly get back up, dust off, and continue on your journey.

I want to transition to another aspect of the concept of 3, 2, 1, 0.

Grandfather

If I had known it'd be the last conversation, what would I have said? Would I have lived in the moment? How is it possible for the days of one to quickly be approaching their end, yet the heart doesn't reach out and grasp all rationality, begging for the words that should have been spoken?

It was my second-to-last college football game at the University of Houston (GO COOGS!). My grandfather and I had drifted apart throughout the years. He had never been to a college game that I'd played in. One would think that the simple fact of his presence would have made me happy. I hadn't seen him in years yet we barely even spoke after the game. I saw him from afar, but allowed my anger for his distance in my life to overcome my excitement at seeing him. I walked up to him and embraced him with a hug. He hugged tightly and whispered to me, "I'm proud of you." I almost shed a tear, simply because I missed him and somewhere deep inside, I wanted to tell him, but I didn't allow myself to; I allowed my pride to control my actions. He looked me in the eyes and said, "I should have supported you more, I should have caught more games, living in the same city and all." Because of my pride, I pretended as though I was unaffected by his admittance of guilt for not being there for me. We departed and as I was about forty feet away, he called me and said, "Pierre, I love you."

"Love you too," I replied nonchalantly.

This would soon become one of my largest regrets in life.

I walked away that night angry. I had been reminded that he hadn't been there when I needed him. I didn't allow myself to see what was really happening. Hugging me tight, telling me he was proud of me, apologizing for not being there, and telling me he loved me...looking back now, could it have been my grandfather was trying to tell me something? Yes. Yes, he was, but I was blinded by the past, which couldn't let me appreciate the present or see the future.

That was the last conversation we ever had—my grandfather died of pancreatic cancer months later.

I hadn't lived in the moment; I'd allowed the past to dictate my present, which in turn left me with regret. People, this is the aspect of 3, 2, 1, 0, that is very important to me. We can no longer allow pride, past hurts, anger, or past situations to halt us from doing or saying the things we should. We have to forgive and let go of the past or it will hold us captive and we will miss the opportunities of our lifetime within 3, 2, 1, 0... Instead of being prideful and angry I should have embraced my grandfather, accepted his apology and moved on together with him. I never took advantage of the opportunity, so please allow me to now:

> Grandpa, I know it's late, but I'm glad you made it to the game that night. I don't care about the other games, I'm just glad you were at that one. I forgive you for not being there, but more importantly I'm doing the best with the memories we had together. I'm doing well, I graduated and have travelled the world, and now I'm sharing my story and the lessons I learned from

you with the world. I love you and I will never forget you. I'm sorry for not saying this before, but please hear it now.

I love you and rest in peace.

I've said multiple times throughout this book that our lives are finite, and so the last aspect of "3, 2, 1, 0," that is vital, is to know that those we love around us won't always be with us. So that we are not forced to say our last words in written form, give your parents, grandparents, loved ones, children, siblings, and all those that are dear to your heart…give them flowers while they are alive. Fill their lives with fragrances of love, cherishing every moment they exist on this earth. It's unfortunate at times but the fact is, one day we will all hit "0," so cherish the "3, 2, 1s" with your loved ones.

Live, my friends.

THE WHITE SIDE
OF THE CLOUD

Perception

As we near the ending of our journey together, I've often wondered how the phoenix, this book, would conclude. Would I know when it was time to stop writing? Would there be a sign, or would I simply just put down the pen? Prior to the book's completion, I found myself aboard a very interesting flight from Rome, Italy to Atlanta, Georgia. As on many flights before, there I was routinely gazing out the window in hopes of slipping off into a beautiful sunset and getting lost in all the charm it had to offer its usual mile-high friend. In all my travels, I'd always found pleasure in obtaining revelations or that sense of peace one receives by simply viewing and acknowledging the beauty of the creator's creations.

"Ladies and gentlemen, we are now making our initial descent into the Atlanta Hartsfield Jackson Airport. Flight attendants please prepare the cabin for landing."

It was just another routine flight where I found myself sitting in the window seat. Maybe I had gotten tired of having the refreshment carts clip my shins, mangle my toes, or even the worst experience, become simply exhausted with row mates who frequented the lavatory so often that it almost made me write CEOs of airlines to suggest forced restroom usage prior to boarding flights. But I digress.

Whilst on board, I found myself just reflecting over the years and experiences it had taken for this book to come to fruition. I had started writing it about three years prior to this point, yet I hadn't felt like I had completed it. That is until the captain began to speak. How so, you might be wondering.

When the captain began to make his routine speech, I paused my "thinking" music to listen in on the announcement, regardless of the fact that this was my sixty-seventh flight segment of the year. Reflecting back on this moment, I can truly say I became appreciative of the routine portions of life. A revelation hit me just as Captain Hagan was making his announcement.

As I was looking out the window, I found myself witnessing one of the most beautiful sights I'd ever seen. There were fluffy, pearly-white clouds as far as the eye could see. It was nearing six p.m. and the sun had begun to set, but it was positioned just right in the sky to provide a kaleidoscope of colors to be individually interpreted by each patron aboard. This beautiful sight, amplified by the setting sun was just vibrant enough to deter a direct stare, yet forgiving enough to invite an off-angle view of the harmonious array of lights surrounding its core. The wonders of retinal excitement could be softly heard throughout the cabin. This is a sight one considers himself lucky, blessed, or just astonished to be a part of—something only comparable to the northern lights of Alaska. The gases of Earth's atmosphere had mixed with what appeared to be vapors from beyond our world, the heavens, to create a myriad of unimaginably picturesque footprints on the sky. Simply put it was beautiful. For at that moment, I was lost in the beauty of my perception of Earth's existence.

Captain Mark Hagan continued, *"Ladies and gentlemen, we are making our final descent into the Atlanta Hartsfield-Jackson Airport. Weather on the ground is approximately sixty degrees, cool winds out of the northeast, and it's overcast with light showers. Flight attendants please prepare the cabin for landing."*

Wait, these were all the variables for a gloomy day in Atlanta, I thought. I found myself baffled, because I was hearing that we were landing in "not so beautiful" weather, yet my perception currently existed in the utopian skies within the same moment in time. As we began our final descent, my perception slowly changed regarding the beauty I was witnessing above the clouds. Then it hit me.

Here I was on the same planet, within the same time zone, and only about 5000 feet of separation determined my perception of beauty. I decided to introduce this brief thought to you all because it is so evident in our daily lives. This brief moment in time taught me that regardless of trials faced, daily tests, or moments of necessary growth, you should keep in mind that you have a choice to perceive your surroundings or situation as being above the cloud amongst the spectacle or below the white of the cloud into your perceived gloomy, cloudy skies. Even the perceived gloom that we landed in, without the dark clouds and the rain, we'd never be able to experience and enjoy those sunny days, that array of color blanketing the sky, or even the ice-chilling blue skies.

Remember: *"Where choice meets perception is either beauty or gloom—either way it's up to you."*

As you soar through life, sometimes it may appear that an uncontrollable element, Captain Hagan in this example, will be the determinant of what you witness, experience, or visualize. But remember; only you can control the perception of what you witness, experience, or visualize.

The beauty is not in the clouds, but rather in the perception.

A NEW NORMAL

"In times of difficulty or difficult decisions, it is prudent to consider the moments in your life where you did not believe you would make it out of sure peril, and then proceed to making your decisions. Combining the fact that you not only survived your unforeseen apocalypse, but you also excelled through that moment. You in fact at that moment, created a new normal." –Pompous Scone, inspired by Tica

As we near the end of our journey together, I find myself amazed at the path life chose to take us down. Think about when you first began reading this book. What caused you to pick it up? What life situations were you dealing with at the time? Which troublesome or glorious situations came and went throughout the course of our journey together?

Now granted, some of you picked up this book because I told you to, others heard about this book from someone they trusted, and surely some of you picked up this book on accident thinking it would divulge the previous hundred sightings of the phoenix fowl. To the latter few, I deeply apologize, but seriously I would like each of you to reflect for a moment back on your own personal journeys while I paint you a mental picture.

A New Normal: My Path

I began writing this book in San Francisco, California. At the time, I had moved to California for work, though I had never crossed the Golden State lines. Nonetheless with two suitcases and about eight hundred dollars in my account, I made the move, not knowing all I'd face. A new state, a new city, few to no friends, and from a political standpoint, California was one hundred percent opposite of everything I had heard as a child growing up in the red state of Texas. Simply put, I found myself questioning my state of normal.

What is the essence of this thing we have come to know as normal? Does something become "normal" because it is widely accepted? Does it become normal by virtue of force? Does one's introduction of something rogue combined with patience allow for an eventual transformation to normal?

Well, when we think about this concept of normal, we see that there are varying definitions and exceptions to that which we deem normal. In my humble opinion, my experience has led me to believe that our normal is actually a combination of what we believe, what we work toward, what we accomplish, and what we allow to occur within our lives, but most importantly, by what we take ownership of and decide to control in our lives.

A year and a half went by in California, and I pretty much lived a solitary life; work and then home to four walls. Initially, out of pure boredom and then by taking the advice of some of the previous chapters, I decided it was time to make a change. I ventured out and began to make friends; some of whom I am still very close to today. I also began to devote more time to the completion of this book. You see, sometimes it takes the encouragement of others to move you forward, and then at other times in life, the only person who can motivate you in a way that fosters change and growth is the person you see in the mirror daily. Thinking of my life at that time, I felt as though some of my experiences combined with the experience of others could benefit the world or those being faced with similar issues; so, I wrote and wrote some more.

Make no mistake though, up until this point of deciding to create a new normal and a new life in California, it had been hell on Earth for me. But this is the primary reason for this chapter. I hope that throughout this journey we have all found what it takes to accept both good and bad in life, and to live strong while leaving our legacies on this earth. In order to accomplish this feat, we will often have to reinvent normal. "So why hell on Earth?" you might ask.

Have you ever woken up and wondered, "What the hell am I doing with my life?" If you haven't, you should return this book. However, if you have felt this way, if even for a moment, you should know that this moment is and will be forever critical to the creation of your legacy. I recall feeling that way while I was in California, until I made the conscious effort to create a new normal and change what I deemed as the norm.

Ponder this quote:

"Sometimes it's as simple as waking up, getting out of bed, and living that day... Sometimes."

This quote is special to me because when we are forced to create a new normal, usually it is during or after a tumultuous occurrence or a series of occurrences. We will deal with this idea of "turmoil" later, but first let me add some color to the origin of this idea of a new normal.

I began to write, creating a new normal, and pulling myself out of my self-perceived slump. Specifically, as the quote said, I found myself waking up, getting out of bed, and living to the best of my ability that day. It worked. My entire mindset about my station in life had been altered by the conscious effort of creating this new normal.

I lived in California for three more glorious years, and enjoyed so much growth purely because I changed my outlook and focused on creating my new normal. Then, it was time for life to provide me with more growth. Life had decided that all California could offer to my growth was nearing its end.

I moved again, this time to Dallas, Texas. I was positioned directly in the heart of Dallas; Uptown Dallas. Applying my lesson of creating a new normal, I continued to write.

(Side Note) Uptown Dallas is an area known as the location for housing the "$30,000 millionaires. This concept is defined as someone putting on an air of riches simply to appear as an elitist or social guru when their means would scream otherwise. This was one hundred percent opposite of the way I had grown up; yet now I was residing there.

What great life lesson would I learn here? Sure, I had my hesitations, but nonetheless the experience would teach me many values that I still hold to this day. I was home again in Texas, though due to my career, during 2012 I spent two hundred and seventy nights in a hotel.

With my new career role demanding so much travel, one would think the top two lessons to be learned in my new environment would have been either, "the beauty of climbing the corporate ladder whilst in mid-twenties," or "how to live within a very pretentious location while yet maintaining one's integrity." Both are sensible possibilities, but neither measure up to the true lesson learned in Uptown Dallas. Unbeknownst to me, in the midst of this social cesspool, a new normal was being created.

This is important because we often have to evaluate our normal to ensure it is beneficial. I learned from this experience that I had begun to prioritize work over family...family that had and would always be there for me. It was critical that the learning continued.

I had to learn to prioritize and cherish the things that were most important in life; family and love. I quickly learned that for someone trying to take his or her place in the corporate arena, the important things in life could easily be overlooked by a life of work, work, and more work.

You see, throughout our journeys of creating a new normal, we must keep our eyes open to the lessons that need to be learned at our various junctures in life. When I was a child, my father and I were extremely close. Though he never missed one of my collegiate football games, provided my very own standing ovations at every band recital, and ensured that every need growing up was met, we drifted apart during this time. This separation was driven by my love for my career, my desire to be promoted quickly, and my overall lack of focus on what was truly important in life. You see, life has a way of constantly teaching us the curriculum needed for us to achieve self-growth...assuming we actually attend class.

"You never know... you should cherish your family because if you should pass away, your company can and will easily replace you, but your family will think and remember every moment of your life. The pain of you being gone will never escape their hearts; Son that is what's important in life. Work and money will

always come and go, but family, love, and friends will be there past the end."

This wisdom was imparted to me by a random guy at a hotel while I was away on one of my business trips. This seemingly simple piece of wisdom, allowed me to realize that my focus was off and it was time to continue this journey toward growth and a new normal.

So why do I keep using this phrase "New Normal"?

"Normal" by definition means conforming to a standard; something usual, typical or expected.

"New" by definition means something that hasn't existed before; something made or introduced or discovered recently.

On the surface level, the phrase, "New Normal," would appear contradictory since "normal" denotes something that is typical or expected; while "new" denotes something that has never existed before. In fact, my friends, this is exactly what I want you to do. Through consistent evaluation, we should contradict ourselves … ….

What in the world is he talking about??????

What I mean is this. Throughout each of your journeys, in order to create the legacies we have discussed, we must always evaluate our situations, both challenging and simple and discover new standards that promote growth. We must nurture this new standard and strive to perfect it, until it is time to introduce the next "new" in our lives, which will set another new standard and allow growth.

Are you starting to see a trend here?

For example:

Golfers, even those who have won many tournaments, often attest to the number of times they have altered their swings. When asked why, the answer is generally the same. "I altered my swing in order to better my game." This is important to note because one might think if you are winning, why change?" Additionally, we often see golfers enter slumps during these "altering swing transitions." The reason is quite simple. They change because they are consistently searching for the next discovery that will yield the expectations of continued success.

Personally speaking, I had to take on a new city and state as well as leave family and friends, all so I could learn a new side of business while learning what it was like to be a hundred percent away from "the nest." But my journey wasn't over; it wouldn't end there. Moving home to Dallas, I would later realize, was ever so critical to my continued growth. The universe knew it was time to learn. The lesson here was time management and prioritization, but most importantly I needed to relearn what was important in life; family and love.

All while writing this book, I would come to see that the creation of this new normal was and had to be a continuing process.

With no surprise here, I moved again. This time it was from Dallas, Texas to Atlanta, Georgia. Here is where it all finally came full circle for me. Through my own journey, I had now learned and knew what to expect when moving away from everything familiar. From previous learning, I knew what it would be like living in a place without family and without friends. I had learned to combine effective time management with a keen focus on work-life balance. Now it was time to put all of it into action. This was all in an effort to create…say it with me, "a new normal." This is important because as we discovered in previous chapters, true growth will start by seeing the issue, taking the necessary steps to remedy the issue, learning from the past mistakes, and then making a conscious effort to change your present into a new normal.

That was a snapshot of my journey with this book.

I'd like everyone reading to take the time to revisit your journey thus far. You see, like the phoenix, the journey is never complete; it must only be developed and grown to its next phase. This, my friends, is the beauty of life. If we take on these growth opportunities boldly and without wavering; when it's all said and done your legacy will persist decades after you are gone.

Earlier, I spoke to turmoil and promised we would revisit this issue. This is very critical to the longevity of one's legacy, because how you view and face turmoil will determine actions that elicit lasting consequences.

A New Normal: Turmoil

"Turmoil. What is its essence? What is its meaning? What is its fragrance? Can it be depicted by the masses once it has reached its faintest stage? Does it mourn its own travail or simply bask in the path it lays before others? Tis fact that since the dawn of ages, men have pondered the Alpha, the Midst, and the Omega of her; yet few have understood the existence and purpose of what is deemed turmoil.

The feeling of turmoil… When a broken heart is as real as an infant's expanding diaphragm taking its first breath into this world.

Turmoil. She embeds under your skin, burrows into the depths of your soul, lying stagnant until hope has convinced you that you are past her; that she has evaporated into the abyss of a dream… But there she is, lying still as the serpent would, urging and tantalizing his prey to cross into his realm of a looming, venomous strike of proximity. We hate her, fight against her, run as far and as long as we can, all in an effort to escape her inevitability. Crushing dreams and hopes of thriving, she whirls through towns and cities destroying everything in her path. From homes to hearts, lives to loves, all with nary an ending in sight. On, forward, forward she whisks, for it is destiny that drives her not knowledge, reason, or even chance. She must go as she will go, for it is will that hath determined her will. For this is her destiny. As the hummingbird sets not a plan for its year of pollinating flight, neither does turmoil in her sporadic evolutionary gust of destruction."-Pompous Scone

This personification of turmoil is one that took me quite a while to grasp simply because I too am human and have felt the welts of turmoil. My friends, what I want each of you to take out of this chapter is that nothing in life worth fighting for or worth dying for will come easy. This undeniable fact will continue to hold true even in your lives as you start that new business venture, as you go back to school to earn that master's degree, as you decide to keep the child without being certain of how you will even afford to bring a child into this world.

Keep this in mind—as you face your turmoil, you will fail and you will make wrong choices, some of which will be irreversible, but in those moments, you must wait patiently and ride out the storm, for it is that very turmoil that will assist you in creating your new normal.

A New Normal:
Cloudy with a Chance of Turmoil

As we have discussed, I have rarely seen gold purged without the introduction of extreme temperatures, nor muscles grown without being first strained, torn, or broken down. By this, I submit that in order for growth to occur, either personal, financial, or mental, turmoil must be present as it is often the catalyst that leads to sustained growth. It is the independent variable that is needed to foster an equation of success; the mortar to uphold your newly created foundation of resilience.

"John, If I had never been fired and faced that entire lay-off process, I would have never had the opportunity to meet you. You are my best friend and I never thought I would be so happy to have been fired just two years ago. You have been my lifeline for these last two years and I have no earthly idea how I ever lived without you. I love you." –Jane Kelly

"Jane, I never thought a woman could understand me in ways that you do. Anytime something of note occurs throughout my day, I immediately think of you, because you are my sounding board. When you are away, I am happier than ever because I know that you are thinking of me, yet I am at my saddest because I miss your presence. I too could not be happier to have faced the pain of losing what I perceived as love, because without it, I would have never walked into your path. I love you." -John O'Malley

I digress, but while I was writing this chapter, two souls destined for love shared their reflections to each other as they focused on how turmoil brought them together. But wait, surely this is unorthodox. The truth is we have all faced moments when a present turmoil has been the unforeseen conduit to a brighter future.

If turmoil is so great, why do we naturally fear her? Why is it that the majority of us reading this very chapter would rather remain constant than to face change in most facets of our lives?

How many of us brushed our teeth this morning, and decided to start on the lower left versus the upper right; our location of choice for the past five, ten, fifteen years? Though very basic, this is a mild change that wouldn't pose too much turmoil for the masses. However, what about other examples where turmoil has crept into our lives unbeknownst to us and we have spent hours, days, months, years, decades even wallowing on the figurative tearing of our muscles—the tearing of our muscles rather than looking into our figurative mirrors and flexing; marveling even at our muscles of personal growth?

A New Normal: The Storm

Within each storm, there is always a period of breakthrough. Said breakthrough however is dependent upon perception. Have you ever stood in the rain and noticed specific rain drops hitting or miss you? Or perhaps you've witnessed someone in the rain, head lowered, walking hastily, and combining zig-zag maneuvering techniques as if their anti-moisture techniques would decrease the amount of rain plopping upon the crowns of their heads. Human nature I guess…

Nonetheless, just as amid a summer Floridian shower, in our lives we face rains of turmoil as the universe attempts to aid in our personal growth. Thankfully, even within these squalls of precipitate learning, there will be breaks in the showers. Unfortunately, one of the problems we "legacy leavers" will face, is that we often are so caught up with dodging the showers and walking hastily to avoid further soakage, that we rarely take the time to see and or appreciate the umbrella of hope a stranger could put above our heads. We're so focused on the turmoil at hand that we rarely pause to be thankful for the brief pause in showers that allow acknowledgment of growth. If we remain vigilant during times of growth, we can free our minds of the purging fires, and alter our focus to how far we have come.

A New Normal:
My Storm and Umbrella of Hope

I was there. I found myself heartbroken and missing "the one," as I had come to know her. Whether it was my pride or her stubbornness, the fact remained that my loving relationship had ended. I'd fought for it, though I have never witnessed a knockout in a title bout with just one fighter. I had to quickly learn that it always takes two to fight for what each one wants, especially when the prize is the same. In any case, I was there.

No psychology or words of affirmation of "who I am" had worked or made it better. It had been months without seeing her face, yet all at once it hit me like a ton of bricks on an ant bed built on a porcelain table. I had to see her. I fought inside. "Don't do it," I exclaimed aloud. My surroundings were perfect for an outburst as I had ventured into the haven of a local Sandestin, Florida bar.

But I didn't listen, no not even to myself. I did not heed my own words. Instead, I opened what I had locked away for months; our photo album. Picture by picture I was destroyed. Suicide by emotional knives being delivered by mine own hands. With the touch of a finger I found myself focusing on the tumultuous storm rather than all the growth and learning that came from mine own turmoil showers.

Subtly, I gazed up and surveyed the room and life was all around me; though in honesty I could only feel the death of love's lost whisper. At this local establishment, laughs and smiles were shared and exchanged, futile conversations were had, drinks were ordered, yet I felt as though I was in a world of one. At that moment, all I could fathom was how much my heart longed for my half, my heart, my love, and my hate. Hate because I hated that I finally had to let her go; hated that I had to accept that she was on a different path; hated that we'd ended when I needed her most. Most of all, I hated how my heart would never allow me to hate her. Though months had passed and countless hours elapsed, I still hated to come to the realization that my love for her remained. At best, nano-seconds had escaped during waking hours where her face did not live within my mind. Essentially, I hated my own love.

You see, love is one of life's greatest lessons for it forces you to learn how to care so much that you would gladly trade your life so that person could exist. Then it teaches you to care for yourself, because the world needs what you will offer it. It concludes its lesson with a curriculum aimed at under-standing that in some amazing way we all are connected with everything that we see or what we choose not to see... So to love one another is to love yourself.

I continued to scroll through the album. With each flick of my finger I thought about the good times, the great moments, the sad moments that brought us closer, the distance that was difficult, the promises made, as well as the promise that was broken:

"I will always be here with you no matter what. We can fight through anything."

In a full and vibrant world, at that moment I'd rarely felt so alone—as if my existence had caved in. Since we had sepa-rated, my entire world reminded me of her. I couldn't listen to music because "we" loved those songs... couldn't say this or that, because "we" used to say those things. I found it hard to exist within the status quo, because my heart still wanted to exist with "we." Simply put, I seriously had no clue of how to move forward and live on. But the saga continued ... Foolishly and unwilling to end the self-inflicted agony, I sought the cause of our dissolution and found there was someone else.

Now, I understand that many of you have also experienced this moment known as the breaking point of love. I was there. It's that moment when you stop running through the rain, because your perceived destination is so far and you are already soaked. It's the moment you say within, "It can't get any worse."

Remember:

"In times of difficulty or difficult decisions, it is prudent to think about the moment in your life where you did not believe you would make it out of sure peril, and then make your decisions. Combining the fact that you not only survived your unforeseen apocalypse, but you also excelled through that moment. You created a new normal"

Finding myself at the apex of hurt, I paid my tab, exited the establishment, and began my march to my hotel, heartbroken, torn, and furious all at the same time. For it was in that moment I realized that it was a year to the day since she had been in my arms. Spending time in the great city of New Orleans for the Fourth of July weekend, we'd gazed into the Cajun sky to witness the freedom fireworks. I'd whispered to her, "I love you" as she clenched my hand tighter. She kissed me and rested her head on my shoulders. Looking up at me, she had whispered amongst the chaos, "I never want to lose you."

Now, a year later, I strolled to my room with no clue of what I'd do upon arrival to remove myself from this state.

A New Normal: Umbrella of Hope

As I walked, I saw an elderly couple about twenty yards ahead, who appeared lost. "Excuse me sir, are you familiar with this place?"

"Not really, but what is it that you are looking for sir?" I replied.

It just so happened that they were on the hunt for the exact building I was staying in. I insisted they let me help, grabbed one of their bags, and asked them to follow me. The man and his wife thanked me and the three of us began our trudge to our lodgings.

He began to make small talk. "So, do you live here? What do you do?"

Being in a "torn" state, I couldn't even see the moment that was unfolding right in front of me. I replied nonchalantly, "I'm from Texas though now I reside in Atlanta. I'm in medical sales management. Yourself?"

"Well we are retired," he replied, "but I'm from Hope, Arkansas. Have you heard of Hope?" he asked.

My eyes immediately watered from the formation of tears. Though he was inquiring about his geographical beginnings, I finally could see what was happening at my lowest moment while I was yet in my "Storm of Turmoil." While my heart felt torn like iceberg lettuce being sliced into a salad, it was "hope" that had found me.

"No sir I haven't heard of Hope, Arkansas, but I'm glad I found you," I replied with tears in my eyes, hidden by the darkness of night.

He chuckled and said, "Well son, I'm glad you found us too. Sometimes in new places, we old folk can wonder around in the dark aimlessly, and the world just has a way of bringing or providing you with the exact help you need at that moment for that situation. You're our beacon."

When we'd arrived at our lodgings and he was thanking me for my assistance, he said, "Well son, we will never be too far from you if you ever need a little hope in your life."

Though we'd only had a cordial exchange of an American nature, that night, metaphorically this man gave me the hope I needed to persevere. He had no clue, but his foreshadowing words held so much meaning for me. He'd given me my moment. It's tough to explain what type of moment or pause in the storm of turmoil that was provided but here it goes:

"It's the time when life is quiet. The wind whistles softly through the coils of your mind, while the blood in your veins whisks to and from your heart. It's the time when you have waited patiently for this instance, with countless hours devoted to patience and decrees of "everything happens for a reason." Speakers have been silenced, time is standing still, and every incline of your storm is leading to this … the moment. This was the moment. The point when tranquility and pain meet opportunity. You're standing at the metaphorical fork yet not allowing the perpetual evolution of Earth's revolution, or the inevitable passage of time to force a decision of left or right.

You're simply living there, then, in that moment. It's the moment when we finally see that to truly live, is to exist outside of accepted existence. In its rawest form, "the moment" is the point when you become stronger than the storm you are enduring, simply because with the assistance of hope you have chosen to be stronger. Let it rain."

You see, "hope" and the universe will never allow you to get lower than you can handle. But it takes vigilance, persistence, and the willingness to overlook the current storm in hopes of walking under an umbrella of hope. Even in pain, hope will always find you to push you forward. Continue walking forward, and creating your new normal.

Dedicated to Hope, Arkansas

THE PHOENIX

There stood the two birds, in utter disbelief at the larger seagull as it swallowed what was left of their meal while flying away. Sitting and watching the epitome of Darwin's survival of the fittest, I'd be astounded at what would take place next. Foodless and empty-bellied, the two wee birds stood on the deck, as though they had come to the end of their roads. Quite honestly, I felt terrible for the two little birds. Here they were, starving, alone, and after patiently awaiting their time to eat, their little morsel of sustenance had been taken away in an instant for no apparent reason.

Sound familiar? Has this ever happened in your life? Has there been time where you waited patiently, took all the proper steps, and due to your persistence, the sun began to shine on your life? Was it a time when the clouds began to disappear and allow the spring-time aura to fill your heart with cheer and hope? Then, in an instant, it's gone and the storms of your life return. The thunder of defeat roars in your skies, while high speed winds of sudden change sweep away any chance of comfort through familiarity. We have all faced this at some point or another, but this, my friends, is when we must apply the principles of "The Flight of the Phoenix." This, as we said earlier, is our crossroad. Will you turn and suffer no more or will you press forward and live forever? Remember, we all have a choice. It is not to say that pressing forward warrants any promise of reward or appeasement, but remember, it is a fact that if we choose to turn and give up… that will be the day we die.

Let's finish the story.

"Squawk Squawk"

As the two little birds stood on the deck, I noticed one bird began to squawk and flutter its wings at the other hungry bird. I don't dare claim to speak the language of birds, but it seemed as though this bird was angry that they'd lost their food to a much larger adversary. He was pointing the finger or in this case, the wing, fussing and expressing his seeming anger to the other bird. What amazed me is that both birds had lost their meal yet only one bird was doing all the squawking and showing his disappointment.

After about two minutes of this fiasco, the angry bird flew away disappointed in the outcome of his patience. It was at that moment I witnessed "The Flight of the Phoenix" in its entirety. I looked on carefully at the little bird that remained, to see what it would do. The whole time I was thinking, *Here is its little crossroad.* The remaining bird stood on the deck for a moment and then took flight back onto the fisherman's boat. Searching the entire vessel for food, the bird seemed more persistent than ever. I watched carefully as I hoped for its persistence's sake, that it'd find at least a small morsel of food to appease its hunger. Minutes went by and nothing was found. There was even a moment the bird appeared as though he had given up. As I observed him walking to the edge of the boat I was sure the bird was going to take flight and give up. But just then, the little bird hopped back down as though something had caught his eye. Intently, I watched the bird's every step, internally rooting for the hungry creature since his persistence cried out for an audience of hope. Then suddenly, out of nowhere, the little bird found food. Tucked away under the fisherman's mid-deck was a small piece of fish that had missed the clearing of the deck as the fisherman was separating the catch. I found myself smiling with excitement for this little, patient, persistent bird.

In about thirty minutes, I had watched this bird face adversity, wait in patience, persist against all odds, press forward at his crossroad, and most of all … it never gave up.

This small creature embodied what I hope we all get from this book.

His "What if," of not having food after it was stolen had to be overcome by his "What is," which was the fact that he still needed to find sustenance and as long as he was still breathing he had a chance to win and accomplish his goal. Unlike the bird that just left squawking, this little bird got out of his own way and didn't allow his anger or disappointment to deter him from the goal at hand. Granted, it probably wasn't the best decision to initially consume their meal out in the open, but now that the damage of the thief had been done, harping on it would only render more hunger pains if not corrected. When the little bird got back on the boat to look for food he had faced defeat and thought of quitting. At this point he ignored the ease of giving up and chose to live, giving it all he had. No regrets remember? Pressing forward, his situation of defeat met its end and he won. He turned impossible into Im-possible.

There is one more key point I want to stress about this story. It is great to persevere in the face of adversity, but unless we learn from our mistakes we will always find ourselves in the same situation. Unlike his last mistake of taking the food on the deck only to have it stolen by a more dominant bird, upon finding food this time, the little bird took his meal into a deep, hidden corner of the boat and enjoyed his meal in secret.

This is the final lesson from the flight. Focus your energy on "What is" while understanding the past. Get out of your own way, and face defeat with the attitude of "I'm still breathing." Also, live life without regrets by allowing your imagination to meet reality. Live every second to the fullest, while learning from every ticking of your clock.

Remember friends, The Flight of the Phoenix is one where we will face peril and pain, but through preparation, patience, perseverance, and constant learning, we will reach our highest potential and soar like the phoenix.

Spread your wings and fly.

ABOUT THE AUTHOR

Having lived a life against all odds, the idea of the Phoenix was born. From being taunted for being an awkward child more interested in books than popularity, to walking on as an undersized Division 1 athlete, and later challenging the status quo in corporate America, Harry Simon, Jr decided that the zest for renewal that continually recreated The Phoenix burned within his own heart. Failure was always supplanted by resolve, losing was a milestone, never to be an end result. Complacency remained the enemy. Understanding The Phoenix was a personal rallying cry that brought Harry from humble beginnings to new heights in each phase of his successful career.

The Phoenix is a mythical creature, but as told in this free-flowing book, it is a life attitude of succeeding against all odds. The storyline is unique, free flowing, authentic and a tribute to a life of never accepting no.

9 781525 545825